CONTENTS

Abbreviations and symbols

adj.	adjective	*AE*	American English	*sb.*	somebody	CD 2	sound file on CD
adv.	adverb	*BE*	British English	*sth.*	something	DVD 1	film or video on DVD
n.	noun	*fml.*	formal				
v.	verb	*infml.*	informal			✕ Extra	additional tasks (optional)

SEQUENCE

01

GOING ABROAD

In today's world, people are going abroad more and more often. This sequence looks at reasons for travelling, how to communicate with people from other countries, and the experience of being abroad.

Interview partners

Activity chest
▶ 5

How often have people in your class been abroad? Use the activity 'Double circles' to interview at least three partners. Introduce your last partner to the class. Use these questions.

- Where were you in your summer holidays? What did you do there?
  I was at home / in Majorca …
  I relaxed … visited … learned …
- Why did you stay at home / go abroad?
  I didn't have the money to … All my friends …
  My family always …
- Have you ever been abroad? Why (not)?
  No, never, because … Yes, I have.
  We often go abroad because …
- Would you like to go abroad more often?
  No, not really, because …
  Yes, because it's a good chance to …

Pair and group work: you will find lots of ideas in the 'Activity chest' at the back of the book

Speak English! und die Welt versteht Dich.

Collect ideas

Activity chest
▶ 13

The pictures at the top of these two pages illustrate some different aspects of the theme 'going abroad'.

nowadays: heutzutage
afford sth.: sich etwas leisten
emigrate: auswandern

1. First work alone. Write down the ideas that come into your mind when you look at the pictures.
2. Compare your ideas with a partner's. Add new ideas or change your ideas.
3. Write sentences and tell the class what you think.

It is easier / harder / (much) more common	to travel / go abroad / visit / live in another country nowadays	than ever before / than in the past	because people can afford to / there are …
Another / A second / One / A further reason	for going abroad	is	to work as / to do / to emigrate / to gain …
Going abroad / overseas	can be	fascinating / a bit scary	because you learn about / get to know / don't know …
When they are abroad	people generally	speak / communicate in …	because …

TOPIC 01

Meeting people

1 An international seminar (A blog)

Every year since 1999, Dr. Elmar-Laurent Borgmann, a German university lecturer at the RheinAhrCampus, Fachhochschule Koblenz, has taken groups of 30 to 40 students from around the EU to seminars on Achill Island, off the west coast of Ireland. These seminars are funded by the EU. Below and on the following pages you will find some extracts from the blog that the students produced.

lecturer: university teacher (Dozent)
Achill: /ˈækɪl/

A Before you read

1. Look at the photos above. Give your first impressions of Achill island. List some words to describe it.
2. Suggest some reasons why international students may come to a seminar like this.
   Perhaps / Maybe they want to …
   They (the students) may come so that they can …

Extract 1_ On Friday 9 February we began our trip from Kaunas, in Lithuania, to Ireland. Happy and excited we were the first group to check into Dublin International Hostel. Students from four other countries in Europe were just about to join us and we simply could not wait to see them all. Finally we were to meet each other face to face after working together since September using the internet.

Evelina Dragunité (Lithuanian group)

6 *just about to:* soon going to

Extract 2_ After a great night in Dublin we left our hostel at noon and headed off to the train station. At the station we had some time to get food and drinks for our four-hour ride to Westport. During the ride people spent the time getting some work done or catching up on some sleep. From Westport to Achill Island we took buses which drove us through an incredible and astonishing landscape. Finally we arrived on the beautiful and 'mysterious' island where we were going to live for the next seven days.

Karsten Kneese (German group)

1 *head off to:* go in the direction of
6 *catch up on sth:* do sth. you couldn't do earlier
9 *astonishing:* hard to believe

Extract 3_ What is the best way to get to know people? One way is to gather everyone in one place and play some games. It is really interesting that different cultures have different rules in the same game, for example in card games. There were also interesting discussions when we talked about the important events that are taking place now in our different countries. We also compared our education systems. Our schools and universities are very different. In the end it was fascinating to talk to different students from different nationalities and we all got to know each other quickly.

Kristina Maria Baraskité (Lithuanian Group)

15 *gather sth./sb.*: collect sth./sb., bring sth./sb. together

Extract 4_ Today the topic of our lunchtime lecture was 'National Stereotypes'. The room was very crowded when students of different nationalities rushed into the room. We had to form national groups, and every group got big pens and little cards. The goal was to discuss the stereotypes which come into our mind when we think of the other countries. So we started to write keywords on our cards and laid them out on the floor. A lively discussion started about the "blonde and blue-eyed Swedish girls", "shy and goulash-loving Hungarians" and "tea-drinking Brits". I think this workshop reminded us that we all have our own stereotypes and that this needn't be something bad. It can actually be an ice-breaker to start a conversation. You only have to keep an open mind for new cultures.

Sabine Rauh (German Group)

30 *lecture*: lesson at a university
31 *rush:* go quickly, hurry
33 *goal:* aim, purpose
44 *keep an open mind:* be ready to accept new ideas

Extract 5_ What do you think about a man sitting on a chair and eating while a woman is kneeling on the floor? This was a part of Janina's and David's role play on Wednesday. The participants had the task of analysing their behaviour and writing down what they saw. "She looks like a slave and I would like to help her," was the interpretation of many students. In fact, Janina and David were playing people from the society of 'Albatros' where women are very highly respected. Men have the duty of tasting all food to make sure it is safe. The woman was kneeling because she wanted to have the most contact to their Goddess of Earth. The message is that it is easy to misunderstand things in another culture. We put on 'cultural glasses'. If we meet strange situations, we shouldn't rush to have a point of view.

Michael Vogel (German group)

5 *behaviour:* way a person behaves, acts
17 *point of view:* opinion

[From: www.rheinahrcampus.de/international/projects/achill2009]

B Understanding the text

Written texts ▶ 1

Written texts ▶ 3.1

1. Scan the text to find the following information. Read quickly and concentrate on finding only the information you need.
   a From which EU country are the students in the picture in Extract 1?
   b Which two methods of transport did the group use to travel from Dublin to Achill? (Extract 2)
   c In Extract 3, after playing some games, what two topics did the students discuss?
   d In Extract 4, where did the students write their keywords about other countries?
   e How are British people described in Extract 4?
   f What are the names of the two students in the picture in Extract 5?
   g What name did these students invent for an imaginary society?
2. Skim the text again quickly. Write a suitable headline for each extract.
3. Read the text again for more detailed information. Make notes under three headings.

FACTUAL INFORMATION (TIMES, DATES, PLACES, ...)	WRITERS' IMPRESSIONS AND FEELINGS	WHAT THE WRITERS LEARNED
- *seminar began 9/2* - ... - ...	- *Lithuanian students "couldn't wait to meet others"*	- *rules for card games ...* - ... - ...

C Analysing the text

Written texts ▶ 2.1

The Achill blog is an example of a 'non-fictional' text. But in which category (or categories) of non-fictional texts does it belong? Classify the text and give your reasons.

Grammar you can use
▶ 1.3

Answers
▶ p. 171

D Check your grammar 1 (The simple past)

Work through the tasks below, then check your answers at the back. Remember that some verbs are irregular and others regular. If you have any problems, go to the grammar summary.

1. Give the correct simple past forms of the verbs.
   - a The students ***were*** (be) excited about the seminar.
   - b The students … (spend) the first night in Dublin. They … (leave) the next morning to travel to the island.
   - c The first part of the journey … (be) by train. Then they … (take) buses.
   - d The students … (play) card games and … (compare) the education systems in their countries. That way, they … (get) to know each other quickly.
   - e The students … (like) their lunchtime lectures and … (rush) into the lecture room.
   - f After writing keywords about stereotypes on cards, the students … (lay) the cards on the floor.
   - g During Janina's and David's role play, the other students … (have) to write down what they … (see) and interpret the meaning of the role play.
2. Look at the sentences in (1) again and make questions.
   - a the students' first night / where? ***Where did the students spend their first night?***
   - b leave / next morning / why?
   - c students / know each other quickly / how?
   - d students / into the lecture room / why?
   - e cards / where?
   - f students / learn / during role play / what?
3. Imagine that sentences a – d in (1) are all wrong. Write them again as negative sentences.
   - a ***The students weren't …***

Grammar you can use
▶ 3.1

E Increase your wordpower (Adjectives ending in –ing and –ed)

Remember that the –ing and –ed forms of verbs can be used as adjectives.

1. Change the verbs in brackets into adjectives and complete the sentences. (All the examples were in the Achill blog.)
   - a (astonish) The landscape of Achill Island is ***astonishing***.
   - b (fascinate) It is always … to meet new people.
   - c (crowd) The room was very … when the students arrived for the lecture.
   - d (drink) The idea of tea- … Brits is a national stereotype.
   - e (respect) Women are highly … in the imaginary society of Albatros.
2. Which form is correct in these sentences?
   - a The book that I am reading right now is very (interesting / interested).
   - b I am (interesting / interested) in foreign countries and their cultures.
   - c When people visit the USA for the first time, they are usually (surprising / surprised) that the country is so large.

2 Are stereotypes 'bad'? (An online article)

You are going to read an article from the BBC News website. It appeared online just before Germany and England played an important football match in London.

A Before you read

Activity chest
▶ 12

Work in a small group to complete tasks 1-3 below. A good activity would be 'Placemats'. Afterwards report to the class.

1. Write down some nationalities (British people, the Germans, ...) and match them to some typical national stereotypes. The adjectives and phrases in the box below will help. (You can find more yourself too.) Use your dictionary if necessary.
   - *The stereotyped image of the British is that ...*
   - *You often hear comments like: "All Italians are ..."*
   - *A common stereotype of Swedish people is that ...*

stereotype (noun)/'steriətaɪp/
a fixed idea that people have about a person, a nation, a place etc. The idea is usually based on very little real information and is often biased or out of date:
racial / sexual stereotypes; common stereotypes of the British are that they all drink tea and wear bowler hats.

ADJECTIVES	PHRASES
aloof • arrogant • boastful • bossy • chaotic • cold • disciplined • disorganised • easygoing • eccentric • emotional • formal • friendly • hard-working • honest • humorous • laid-back • lazy • loud • mean • modest • nationalistic • organised • outgoing • passionate • polite • punctual • quiet • reliable • reserved • romantic • rude • systematic • talkative • tolerant • traditional • warm-hearted	don't like foreigners • drink beer • drink tea • drink wine • eat sauerkraut • eat snails • have great bands and music • have blond hair and blue eyes • have no sense of humour • smoke a lot • wear leather shorts • wear nice / terrible clothes

Written texts
▶ 5.1

2. Where in your opinion do stereotypes come from? For example, from TV programmes that we watch. Make a list of ideas. Put the most important idea at the top of your list.
3. Look at your list of stereotypes and at the advert for a hi-tech German car. Are stereotypes always negative? Explain and give examples.

ARE NATIONAL STEREOTYPES OFFENSIVE ?

It is not offensive to refer to Germans as 'Krauts', according to Britain's advertising watchdog.

The Advertising Standards Agency (ASA) says a leaflet carrying a picture of a German footballer with the slogan: "The Krauts are coming" is "a light-hearted reference to a national stereotype unlikely to cause serious or widespread offence".

The leaflet was produced by a company called Dronco Abrasives in the run-up to the Germany-England world cup qualifier.

Dronco, whose parent company is German, said the term was a "humorous reference to Germans' allegedly high consumption of sauerkraut".

But German cultural attaché, Tilman Hancker, objects to the ruling: "Speaking personally, I would be offended to be called it and I think most people would not find it a very nice name."

What do you think? Is stereotyping okay if it's 'just for fun'? Or should we be more careful about offending other nationalities?

[From: http://news.bbc.co.uk/1/hi/talking_point/1617138.stm] Click here to have your say

1 *offensive:* rude, nasty
2 *advertising watchdog:* organisation checking that advertisements are acceptable
12 *abrasive:* Schleifmittel
13 *run-up (to):* period of time before
15 *allegedly:* angeblich
16 *ruling:* decision

B Understanding the text

Written texts ► 3.1, 3.2

1. Skim quickly through the article. Decide which statement below is the most suitable when describing it. Give a reason for your answer.
   a It gives information about an advert.
   b It tells you about a football match.
   c It asks for your opinion about national stereotypes.
   d It explains that British people often call Germans 'Krauts'.
2. Read the article again in more detail. Complete the sentences below with the missing information. Then outline the main ideas in the article in a few sentences, using your own words as far as possible.
   a The article probably appeared on the BBC News website just before …
   b It tells us about an advertisement which …
   c The ASA in Britain decided that …
   d However, a German diplomat …
   e The article ends with …

C Reacting to the text

Written texts ► 5.2c

Write to the BBC website. Answer the question at the end of the article giving your own ideas about the topic. Write 100 – 150 words.

3 An American view of the Germans
(An interview)

Erin is an American exchange student at the RheinAhrCampus, Fachhochschule Koblenz. In this interview from a podcast, she is talking to one of her teachers about living in Germany.

Highway, central Texas

A Before you listen

CD 1

Activity chest
▶ 13

At home in the USA, Erin is a student at a university in Austin, Texas. Using the pictures on the right, make a list of differences between Texas and Germany that you think Erin might talk about in the interview. Then compare with a partner and finally tell the class your ideas:

- *She perhaps thinks that in America the landscape / cities / … is / are … than in Germany.*
- *She may feel that American people are …*
- *She maybe finds Germans / Germany …*

Downtown Austin

Hi!

B Understanding the text

Sound and (moving) images
▶ 1.2

1. Copy this chart, then listen and finish the notes.
2. Use your notes to give the main ideas in the text orally.
   - *The American student Erin was born …*
   - *She grew up … so …*
   - *When she arrived in Germany, her first impressions were …*
   - *She often feels that in Germany …*

PERSONAL DETAILS
- *born Forth Worth Texas*
- *grew up in the 'military'*
- *travelled a lot*

FIRST IMPRESSIONS
- *arrived Germany 16/02 at first …*
- …

EMOTIONS / FEELINGS
- …

C Reacting to the text

Written texts
▶ 5.1

Talk in class. How do you feel about what Erin says? Do you think her comments about German people are fair? Give your reasons.

[From: http://www.absolutely-intercultural.com/?p=511]

TOPIC 02

Speaking English

lingua franca: a language used for communication between people who individually speak different languages: *English is* a lingua franca *for the international business community.*

Excuse me, Sir. I'm terribly sorry to bother you, but I wonder if you would mind helping me a moment, as long as it's no trouble, of course.

Sign in a hotel in Beijing

bother sb.: jdn. stören

Collect ideas

In a small group, look at the images on this page and together agree on the best way to finish the sentences below. Read your final sentences to the class.

1. English is …
2. A 'lingua franca' is necessary today because …
3. English is the native language in …
4. However, millions more people around the world speak it in order to …
5. It is easy to make mistakes in a foreign language with spelling, …
6. Speaking a language also means knowing about the culture of the country, for example …
7. There are many different ways to practise and improve your English, for example …

1 Global English (A text with facts and figures)

The following text gives some basic facts and figures about global English.

A Before you read

Activity chest
▶ 1, 3

Make notes about the questions below, then use 'Appointments' or 'Bus stop' to find a partner and compare your ideas. Report afterwards to the class.

1. Why, in your opinion, are you learning English at school?
2. How – if at all – do you use English outside your English classroom?
3. What situations can you imagine when you may use English in the future?

The 'three circles' of global English

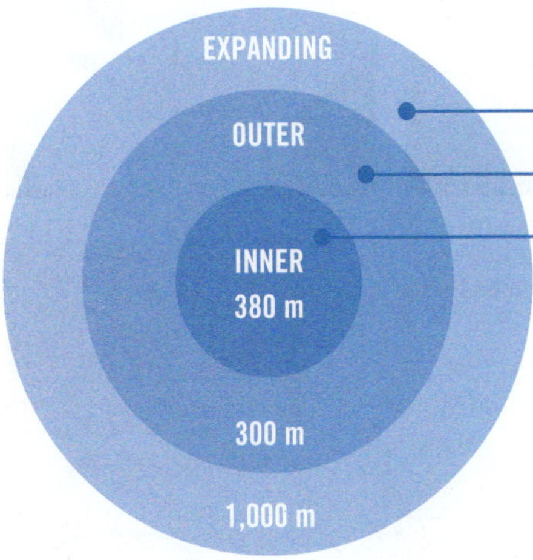

Above - left to right: 1. Times Square, New York 2. An Indian call centre worker helps a customer in the UK with a computer problem 3. A Chinese businessman checks his mobile

Language experts often divide speakers of English into three groups. These groups are represented by three concentric circles.

The INNER circle contains the 380 million native speakers of English in the UK, Ireland, the USA, Australia, New Zealand and parts of Canada. The largest number live in the USA, and it is often said that it is due largely to modern American culture and business that English is so important today.

During the 18th and 19th centuries, Britain established an empire that covered large parts of Africa, India and places in the Far East like Malaysia and Hong Kong. The people who live here today make up the OUTER circle. For them, English is an official (or second) language which is learned at school and used in many everyday situations.

The majority of English speakers, however, are in the EXPANDING circle – 'expanding' because this group is getting bigger all the time. These are people – like you – who learn and use English as a foreign language because it is the global communication tool of business, science, entertainment, the internet and so on. English is currently spoken like this by around 1,000 million – a billion – people, but it is estimated that by around 2050, the language will be spoken (or at least understood) by nearly half the total population of the globe.

2 *represent sth.:* show sth.
2 *concentric:* konzentrisch
5 *due to sth.:* dank
7 *establish sth.:* (here) etwas aufbauen
8 *Far East:* Fernost
16 *currently:* at the moment
16 *billion:* Milliarde (!)
17 *estimate sth.:* etwas schätzen

B Understanding the text

Activity chest
▶ 4

1. Study the text and prepare a 'Cheat sheet'.
2. Use your Cheat sheet to give a short talk about the 'three circles' of global English.

C Analysing the text

Activity chest
▶ 12

Work through the tasks below in a small group. Use a 'Placemat' with an OHP transparency to show your ideas to the class.

Writen texts
▶ 2.1, 4.1

1. In which category (or categories) of non-fictional texts does this text belong? Give your reasons. Where (in books? online? ...?) do you frequently find texts of this type?
2. Look at the diagram at the back of your book called 'Communicating with texts'. Then complete the sentences below about this text in your own words.
   a The writer of the text is (probably) ...
   b The reader is (probably) somebody who ...
   c The writer's intention is to ...
   d The writer uses a diagram in the text: this helps the reader to ...
   e There are also some pictures which illustrate ...
   f The way the writer also divides the text into paragraphs makes it easier for the reader to ...
   g We can say that the language the writer uses in the text is rather ...
   h The effect of this type of language on the reader is ...

✖ **Extra:** Write a short text which summarises these ideas.

D Check your grammar 2 (The passive)

Grammar you can use
▶ 1.10

Answers
▶ p. 172

Work through the tasks below, then check your answers at the back. If you have any problems, go to the grammar summary.

1. Active or passive? Give the correct forms of the verbs.

a Language experts often ... (divide) English-speakers into three groups.
b These groups ... (represent) by three concentric circles.
c English ... (speak) as a native language in Britain and Ireland.
d Australians also ... (speak) English.
e Experts ... (estimate) that half the world's population will know English by 2050.
f It ... (estimate) that half the world's population will know English by 2050.

2. Write these active sentences again as passive sentences.

a People in India speak English. ***English ...***
b Business people use English as a communication tool.
c Half the world's population will speak English one day.
d People often say that English is a difficult language. ***It ...***

2 Rude Germans? (An online magazine article)

Speaking a language correctly is more than a question of grammar and vocabulary. It is also necessary to understand the different culture. The article below looks at one aspect of intercultural communication between Germans and Americans.

A Before you read

Activity chest ▶ 13

Write down some examples of behaviour or language that you think are either 'rude' or 'polite'. Compare with a partner, then share your ideas with the class.

I think it is rude when / I hate it when	people …
A good / Another example of politeness is when	a person / someone …

BRUTALLY HONEST

"Have you gained weight?"

Don't beat around the bush in Germany. If someone asks a question, answer it honestly and expect the same in return. "Yes, I have put on a few pounds," is the correct answer.

You've been invited over to a friend's house, and his grandmother serves you a cake she has labored over for hours.

Granny: I had to go all over town to get the ingredients. It's my own grandmother's fruitcake recipe, but you can't get pickled figs and horseradish syrup at the shops anymore!

You have three responses to choose from:

a) Oh, thank you so much. It looks lovely.
b) Oh, thank you, but I'm dieting. I can't eat cake.
c) I don't like fruitcake at all and figs make me swell up and break into a hideous, oozing rash.

If you picked a), you are probably English or American. And even if you can't stand fruitcake, you'll shovel it in to make granny happy. Many well-mannered (or quick-thinking) Americans may also have chosen b).

The third answer, though, is reserved exclusively for Germans. How, after all, can honesty be rude? Why on earth would you lie? say the Germans. You don't like fruitcake, why pretend that you do? And those figs could kill you!

In England or the US, of course, answer c) could very well result in a rolling pin on the head. In Germany, however, it's merely a standard form that human interaction takes. You say what you have to say and that's that. You meet up with a German friend you haven't seen for a while and chances are he might ask, "Have you gained weight?" It's not meant as an insult, merely a polite inquiry. The bottom line is that the rules of human interaction are different in Germany […]

Contributed by Maria Snyder, now living in Chicago, USA

[From: Spiegel Online: Germany Survival Bible, 18 May 2006]

1 *gain weight:* become heavier
2 *beat around the bush:* speak indirectly
6 *labor over sth.:* work hard to do sth.
7 *pickled figs:* eingelegte Feigen
7 *horseradish:* Meerrettich
13 *break into a hideous oozing rash:* einen scheußlichen, nässenden Ausschlag bekommen
16 *shovel sth. in (infml):* eat quickly
17 *well-mannered:* polite
21 *rolling pin:* Nudelholz
26 *inquiry:* question

B Understanding the text

Activity chest
▶ 8

You are going to look at the text with an activity called 'Freeze-frames'. Work through the tasks below in small groups.

1. Check first that you have understood the main points of the text.
   - How does the first paragraph say you should answer your friend's question? Why?
   - In the story about the cake, which of the three answers can only Germans give? Why?
   - Which of these statements best summarises the writer's point of view at the end?
     a Germans and Americans have different ideas about what is 'rude' or 'polite'.
     b Germans are rude.
     c Americans often tell lies.
     d British and American people are just too polite.
2. In the text, the writer Maria Snyder describes two situations: a German friend who asks if you have gained weight and a visit to a German friend whose grandmother has made a cake.
   - In your group, choose one of the situations and prepare a Freeze-frame tableau. Think about: the characters in the scene; what is happening; how different people in the scene are feeling.
   - Show your Freeze-frame to the class. One of you is a reporter who interviews the characters.

C Analysing the text

Written texts
▶ 2.1, 4.1

1. In which category (or categories) of non-fictional texts does this text belong? Explain your answer and give examples from the text.
2. Where can you frequently find texts of this type? Where did this text appear?
3. Look at the diagram at the back of your book called 'Communicating with texts'. Use the diagram to write a short analysis of the text. Think about the following points:
   - Who is the writer and who are the probable readers?
   - What is the writer's intention?
   - What sort of information / ideas etc. does the reader probably want?
   - How does the writer put across her ideas to the reader? By explaining them in an abstract way in words? By using examples or concrete situations? ...
   - Think about the language in this text. How would you characterise it (formal, complicated, ...)?
   - What is the overall effect of this text on the reader, in your opinion?

Grammar you can use
▶ 1.9 (*by* + gerund)

D Reacting to the text

Written texts
▶ 5.2c

What do you think about the article? Do you agree with the writer? Write a letter or email to the magazine giving your ideas in around 100 words.

3 Improving your English (An internet forum)

The following text and picture are from an internet forum. Users worldwide write in with their opinions, and the common language for everyone is English. This week, someone has started a new thread called: "What's the best way to improve your English?"

A Before you read

What possibilities can you think of for improving your English outside school?

WHAT'S THE BEST WAY TO IMPROVE YOUR ENGLISH?"

Here in the Netherlands I think everybody speaks English quite well. (Sorry! That doesn't sound very modest, but it's true!) Maybe one reason is that we start learning English in school when we're quite young, but I think another reason is that our TV is mostly in English. By that I mean that our programmes aren't dubbed like they are in some other countries – like Germany or France, I think (?). All our movies, shows etc. are in the original English and we have subtitles along the bottom of the screen. Here's a typical screenshot from a TV show here in Holland.

So you see, we get used to hearing Tom Cruise, Julia Roberts or whoever with their proper voices. I'm not saying that if you want to speak English well, you should watch TV all day! But it is certainly one reason why I understand native speakers really easily. SO – what do you all think???

Anton, Amsterdam, the Netherlands

2 *modest:* not saying how good you are
5 *dub sth.:* etwas synchronisieren
9 *get used to sth.:* sich an etwas gewöhnen
11 *proper:* real

B Understanding the text

Written texts ▶ 3.1, 3.2a

Skim the text to get a general idea of its content. Then read it again in more detail. Make notes of the key points, then outline in your own words the writer's main ideas.

C Reacting to the text

Work in groups to continue Anton's thread – that is to say, discuss and write your ideas in reply to what he says.

✕ **Extra:** When everyone has 'posted' their reply, each group can start its own new thread. Pass these on to other groups in a 'Chain writing' activity. Use Anton's text as a model for your text.

TOPIC 03

Working abroad

Au pairs typically live for six – more usually twelve months – with a host family. Their main job is looking after the family's children.

Work camps are normally around four weeks long and bring together volunteers from many different countries to work on a local project. The projects can be in Europe or worldwide.

Work placements (also called 'internships') take place in a company abroad and generally last between three and six months.

work placement (internship): Praktikum

Perhaps after you finish school, you would like to get away and 'see the world'. But that isn't so easy without spending loads of money. There are possibilities, however. You can work as an au pair or as a volunteer at a work camp, or you can do a work placement.

Collect ideas

Activity chest ▶ 13

Work with a partner. Look at the pictures above and collect ideas about working abroad, then report to the class.

1. Why would(n't) you like to work abroad?

Because	I'd like / I want	to meet / to improve / to get to know / to do something different / …
	I don't really want	
	I can't … / my boyfriend (girlfriend / family) … / …	

2. How long would you think of spending abroad?

I'd like	to spend as long as possible abroad.	
I wouldn't want	to stay too long.	
The ideal time	would be	a week / a couple of months /…

3. If you worked abroad, which of the three possibilities on this page would you find most attractive? Why?

I'd like / I'd prefer	to become / to work as / to do a …	because …

4. What would you be afraid of or worried about if you went to work abroad?

I'd be (most) afraid of / worried about	feeling homesick / missing … / feeling … / not understanding … / not getting on with … /…

1 Working as an au pair (A report)

Kristina Bellach from Germany has just come home after working abroad as an au pair. The agency which organised her placement, Internationale Sprach- und Studienreisen, has asked her to write a report for their website.

A Before you read

1. Say what you know already about the work of an au pair.
2. Imagine that next year you will be an au pair. List some questions that you will perhaps have before you go:
   What will my host family be like?
   Where ...?

B Understanding the text

1. Read Kristina's report and make notes under the following headings. Don't look up any words in your dictionary. Just find the key facts.

- how long? - where? - the family she lived in	- the children - things she did when she wasn't working - her feelings at the end of her stay

Written texts ▶ 3.1

2. Read the text again. There are probably some words and phrases you don't understand. Try to work out what they mean. At the end, explain to the class how you worked out the meaning. (For example, other words in the text that helped you).

C Analysing the text

Written texts ▶ 2.1, 2.2h

1. Which of the four main categories of non-fictional text types does this text belong in? Explain your answer.
2. Reports usually have a standard structure as shown below. Explain with examples how Kristina's report follows this structure.

- Heading - Introduction: the subject of the report (what it will be about) - Information arranged in paragraphs – normally one paragraph for each new piece of information - Conclusion and recommendations - Person or people who produced the report

3. Write an analysis of Kristina's report. Think about these points:
   - Why iSt wants Kristina's report on its website.
   - How Kristina writes the report in order to put across her ideas (and help iSt).
   - The probable reader of the report and the effect that Kristina's report has on them.

Au Pair Report: Kristina Bellach (Greater London)

One year, 365 days, 8,760 hours ... How can you summarise one year? Well, I will try to write down everything I learnt, loved and felt during my year as an au pair in South West London.

Looking back from today, back home in Germany, I still can remember everything that happened during my year, and my stay felt rather like a couple of months and not like a year, which I think is a positive thing.

Anyway, on 3rd September last year, I left everything and everyone behind to start over as an au pair in a family I had never met before. Of course, saying goodbye to the people you love is never easy but to me, it was rather like fulfilling a dream because I love England, its people and culture.

I arrived at Heathrow airport and I spotted the faces of the family I knew from the application forms. Puuuuh, what a feeling! What do I have to do next? What do they think? I had thousands of thoughts running through my head, but before I could say anything, they gave me a big hug and kiss and said "Welcome to England!" I was literally overwhelmed by all the warmth and love I was given.

From day one I got more used to my new surroundings and I adjusted to my host family's life. What can I say? It all worked out from the very beginning. I spent lots of time with the children, Tom (3) and Martha (6), but also with the parents, Kate and Martin. After a while I found myself talking about my host parents as my real parents, and I was stunned by that. It just happened, but I still knew that I only had one brother, one mother and one father and they lived in Germany.

It is a huge responsibility to look after two children who aren't yours, but the more you spend time with them at the playground, in the city or even in the house, the more you start to see them as a part of yourself, and you want to protect them no matter what.

My task as au pair was divided into childcare (20–25 hours/week) and cleaning (3-4 hours/week) which was, I thought, a fair and well-organized schedule. I had lots of spare time which I spent with friends, I did language courses at a college, and I went on several trips to other parts of England, such as Bath, Brighton, Liverpool, Manchester, Oxford, Cambridge, Birmingham, etc.

I know you have probably heard this before, but I had the time of my life: it was a year I will NEVER forget. I made lots of new friends, saw lots of different places and, lucky me, I was able to stay with a family that was the best host family you can ever think of. Thanks, iSt!

However, as you can imagine, working as an au pair doesn't last forever, so you come to the point when you have to say goodbye to the people you love, people you have got to know and to love during one year. When I left, the older girl started crying and it really touched me. I felt like I was letting someone down, although I know that wasn't true.

Although I'm still having some difficulties getting back into my old life before I was an au pair, I can recommend it to everyone! Please do it, it's a unique experience. You will never experience anything like it again.

[From: Kristina Bellach / iSt Internationale Sprach- und Studienreisen GmbH]

2 Volunteering abroad (A promotional video)

You find this video on the website of an organisation called Cross-Cultural Solutions.

DVD 1

A Before you watch

1. What does the title above the photo tell you about the video?
2. What do you think may be happening in the still?
3. What impression of volunteering do you get from the still? Why?

still: Standbild

B Understanding the video

Work in a small group.

Sound and (moving) images ▶ 1.2

1. Watch the video and develop a 'Listening grid'. Compare grids in your group, agree on one final grid, then watch and take notes.
2. Compare notes, then outline orally the main points of the video. Explain:
   a why the placement was good for Will (what he learned etc.),
   b why it was also good for his Chinese hosts.

The volunteer in this video is	… *(name)*, a volunteer …
The video shows us that	the placement was good for Will because …
During his time there,	Will …
Will's placement was also good for his Chinese hosts, however, because …	
Will's hosts (including the Buddhist monk) …	

C Analysing the video

Activity chest ▶ 12

Work in your group again to answer the following questions. You could use a 'Placemat'. Report to the class afterwards.

Written texts ▶ 2.1

1. Which of the non-fictional text types is this video an example of? Explain your answer with examples.
2. How can this video give us an idea of Will's experiences that would not be possible with a written text? Use the expressions in the box in your answer.

> written • (printed) texts • videos • words • photographs / illustrations • moving images • sound • to show / describe • the reader can … • the viewer can … • the advantage of written texts / videos is that …

D Write about the video

Write answers to both questions (100-200 words each).

1. (Comprehension) Outline the main points of the video.
2. (Analysis) Explain the purpose of the video and describe how it achieves its aims.

[From: Cross-Cultural Solutions, New York]

3 A work camp (A podcast)

Last year, Stefanie from Germany and Jonathan from England were volunteers at a work camp in Nepal. You are going to listen to a podcast about their experiences.

A Before you listen

CD 2

The expressions below will help you when you listen to the podcast. Using the map above and your own ideas, match the expressions and the definitions, then compare with a partner.

EXPRESSIONS	DEFINITIONS
community centre • crops • Everest • Gatlang • Kathmandu • monsoon season • Nepalese • rewarding • long (for sth.) • trek (noun)	adjective from Nepal (the ~ people) • capital of Nepal • giving you a feeling that you have done sth. good • long, often difficult walk • place where everyone from an area can go • plants grown for food • small village in Nepal • time of year when it rains heavily • want (sth.) very much • world's highest mountain

B Understanding the podcast

Sound and (moving) images ► 1.2
Written texts ► 3.2

1. Work in a small group. Listen to the podcast to get a general idea of its content. Stefanie and Jonathan divide it into four parts. Note down their four headings.
2. Divide the headings among the members of your group so that each person listens for different information. Listen and takes notes under your heading(s).
3. Use all your group's notes to summarise in your own words what you learned.

C Reacting to the podcast

Written texts ► 5.2e

Write one of the following. It will help you to find any extra information you need if you can go online.

1. Imagine that you have just been an au pair abroad. Write a report of your experiences there.
   Or: Imagine you are an au pair at the moment. Write a diary about a typical day.
2. Imagine that you have just been a volunteer at a work camp abroad. Write a report about your experiences.
   Or: Imagine that you are at a work camp at the moment. Write a diary about your typical day.

4 A work placement in the UK (An advertisement and a formal letter)

management assistant: Kauffrau/Kaufmann

After her Abitur this year, Anja plans to train as a management assistant. But first, she wants to do a work placement in the UK.

A Before you read

Activity chest ▶ 2

Anja is looking online at advertisements for work placements. Brainstorm questions she will have in mind when looking. For example: ***What job? Where? …?***

B Understanding the advertisement

Written texts ▶ 3.1

Scan the advertisement below for answers to your questions in A. Don't use your dictionary. Try to guess unknown words from the context.

WORK PLACEMENTS IN THE UK: COVENTRY AIRPORT

Coventry Airport is a small but fast-growing international airport situated in the centre of England. We are pleased to offer work placements to EU students and we are currently looking for young people aged between 18 and 25 to work in our airport offices. Internships are available for 3 or 6 months. Duties will include routine office work such as answering the telephone, filing documents and some correspondence. No previous experience of office work is necessary, but applicants must have excellent computer skills and a good knowledge of English. We are also looking for people who are friendly, reliable and keen to learn. Accommodation is available at an international student hostel 1 kilometer from the airport. Interns will receive a monthly wage of 450€.

How to apply

If you are interested in a work placement with us, please download and fill in the application form on our website www.coventryairport.co.uk and send it with a letter of application to: Amanda Griggs, Coventry Airport, Coventry CV4 8QT, UK

C Complete the letter

Written texts ▶ 2.2d

You can see the letter that Anja wrote on the next page. Complete it with the phrases in the box, then compare with a partner.

a good knowledge of • I would like to apply for one • Yours sincerely • I would very much welcome the opportunity • look forward to hearing from you soon • my Abitur qualification in May this year • My employers there • Dear Ms Griggs • on the 'ichsuche_einpraktikum.de' website • 27 January 20 _ _

Alter Postweg 21
51107 Cologne
GERMANY

Ms Amanda Griggs
Coventry Airport
Coventry CV4 8QT
UK

(1) ....

(2) ....

Application for a work placement

(3) .... of the work placements which you advertised (4) .... I would be interested in a six month placement. I would be available to start work in August this year.

I am currently studying for my Abitur ('A' Levels) in the sixth form of a school in Cologne, Germany. I hope to obtain (5) ....

As you will see from my enclosed application form, I have excellent computer skills and (6) .... English. I have no formal training in office work, but earlier in my school career I did a two-week work placement in a local company. (7) .... found me friendly, reliable and keen to learn. (8) .... to work in an international airport and believe I would be an enthusiastic and hard-working employee. I hope that you will consider my application and (9) ....

(10) ....

Anja Stadler

Encl.: Application form

D Reacting to the texts (Creative writing)

Written texts
▶ 5.2e

Work in small groups.

1. Look at the advertisement on the last page. Using it as a model, write an advertisement for another work placement. Invent the details yourselves.
2. Swap your advertisements in class so that each group has an advertisement from another group. Write a reply to the advertisement using Anja's letter as a model.
3. Make a classroom display of your advertisements and letters.

E Check your grammar 3 (going to / will)

Grammar you can use
▶ 1.4
Answers:
▶ p. 172

Work through the task below, then check your answers at the back.
If you have any problems, go to the grammar summary.

Complete these sentences with the correct form.

a I ***will be*** (be) 17 next birthday.
b What ... (you / do) after you leave school? Do you have any plans yet?
c I saw an advertisement for a work placement in a newspaper yesterday.
- ... (you / apply) for it?
d My new job starts next week. I'm really excited. I think it ... (be) great.
e I hope my new boss ... (be) nice.
f I've just got a work placement in Spain. The problem is, I don't speak Spanish so I ... (learn) it before I go.
g Where ... (you / live) while you're on your work placement?
- The agency finds host families for all its interns. I got a letter about my family this morning. I ... (have) a room in their flat in the centre of town.
h Everybody should make the best of their time abroad. I have lots of plans for things to do in England. I ... (visit) London. I ... (also / go) to Scotland and Wales if I can. And, of course, I ... (eat) lots of fish and chips.
i Where's Peter?
- I don't know, but I expect ... (come) soon.

F Increase your wordpower (Word families)

Grammar you can use
▶ 3.1

1. Complete the grid below. Use your dictionary if necessary.
2. Practise writing sentences with the word pairs. Use your dictionary to help you.
For example:
*What is the **difference** between formal and informal letters?*
*Formal and informal letters are quite **different**.*

ADJECTIVE	NOUN	VERB	NOUN
important	*importance*	*advertise*	*advertisement*
different	...	*inform*	...
excellent	...	*apply*	...
reliable	...	*communicate*	...
homesick	...	*decide*	...
possible	...	*arrange*	...
responsible	...	*discuss*	...
difficult	...	*introduce*	...
happy	...	*explain*	...
lucky	...	*qualify*	...
enthusiastic	...	*know*	...
fictional	...	*experience*	...
friendly	...	*summarise*	...

TOPIC 04

Settling abroad

settle (verb): go to live somewhere, especially permanently:
They left Britain and settled in America.

Settling abroad – 'emigrating' – is not like working abroad for a short while. It is something probably permanent. For individuals and families who decide to start a new life in a new country, it involves making some life-changing decisions.

Collect ideas

SWOT diagrams are routinely used in the business world to help make important decisions, but they are a useful tool for personal decisions, too.

	Positive	Negative
Personal influences	S Strengths	W Weaknesses
Outside influences	O Opportunities	T Threats

SWOT ANALYSIS
S = Strengths: the positive aspects of your personality; things you can do.
W = Weaknesses: the negative aspects of your personality; things you are not good at.
O = Opportunities: those (good) things which you may achieve if everything goes well.
T = Threats: factors which may make it hard to succeed.

1. Work in a group. Imagine that you are thinking of emigrating – either as individuals or a family. Draw a blank SWOT diagram on a piece of paper. Look at the four statements below. Decide where they belong on the diagram and write them in.
   a We speak the language of the new country. (STRENGTH)
   b We may find when we arrive that people are unfriendly.
   c We often feel homesick when we're away from home.
   d We may take up new hobbies in the new country.
2. Brainstorm more ideas and write in the statements.
3. Make a poster of your final SWOT diagram and show it to the class.

Activity chest ▶ 2

1 Greetings from abroad (Mediation)

The text on the next page is from the Kabel eins website. In it, a family who has emigrated to New Zealand sends greetings and reports how things are going after six months. A New Zealand friend is staying with you in Germany at the moment. You are looking at the website and your friend is interested to know what the text says.

Activity chest ▶ 2
Working in groups and on projects ▶ 2

A Before you begin

Work with a partner or in a small group and brainstorm ideas about the questions below. Then share your ideas with the class.

1. Imagine that a family is spending its first six months in a foreign country. Note down what aspects of life there may be important:
   a for the parents, b for the children, c for the whole family.

They may find that	the people / the weather / ...	is / are not as ... as they imagined.
They may	underestimate / overestimate	the ... how easy it is to ...
They may be	(pleasantly) surprised / disappointed / discouraged	by ...
They may find it	easier / harder	to ... than they expected.

under-/overestimate sth./sb.: etwas/jdn. unter-/überschätzen
discouraged: entmutigt
foresee sth.: etwas vorhersehen

2. Before people emigrate, they obviously try to plan their new life, and to find out as much as they can about their new homeland. But they can't foresee everything, and some things they can only guess. Other things may not work out as planned. Speculate about some examples.

B Explain to your friend

With a partner, take half of the text each and explain it in English to your New Zealand friend.

Written texts ▶ 5.1

C Reacting to the text

Discuss the Kux family's experiences starting a new life abroad:
- What went well for the family? Why?
- What didn't go so well? Why?

✕ **Extra:** Use this family's experiences to write a list of tips for people who are thinking of emigrating.

Grüsse von der Familie Kux aus Neuseeland Hallo Kabel eins, Nach fast 6 Monaten nun viele Grüße aus dem schönen Kiwiland!

Im Moment befinden wir uns im tiefsten Winter und Christchurch ist von den 5 „großen" Städten NZs die kälteste. Das heißt, auf Grund der meist schlecht isolierten Häuser, wie z.B. unseres, haben wir im Schnitt 8–12 °C in den Räumen und trotzdem hohe Stromkosten für die nachträglich gekauften Elektroheizungen.

Aber wir haben gehört, dass auch verwöhnte Europäer sich nach ein paar Jahren an diese Temperaturen gewöhnen und dann, wie die Kiwis, mit Mütze, Anorak und kurzen Hosen durch den Schnee laufen können.

Ansonsten ist der Winter hier unglaublich, mal schneit und regnet es und dann scheint die Sonne und ein warmer Wind aus der Südsee hebt die Temperaturen um 10–15 °C. Die Pflanzen scheinen sich mit den Jahreszeiten auch nicht so recht auszukennen. Die Laubbäume schmeißen brav ihre Blätter ab, es ist ja Winter, aber die Blumen, Vögel und Schmetterlinge scheint das nicht zu stören.

Unsere Familie hat sich gut eingelebt, Thomas ist sehr zufrieden mit seinem Job und ich arbeite zur Zeit ein paar Stunden pro Woche in einem Alten- und Pflegeheim.

Unsere Schulkinder haben sich gut integriert, auch die Schuluniform ist kein Problem mehr! Sie sind jetzt alle schon in einer normalen Kiwiklasse und gerade gab es Halbjahreszeugnisse, mit denen wir sehr zufrieden sind. Das haben wir sicher auch der tollen Schule und den engagierten Lehrern zu verdanken. Das Schulsystem ist anders als bei uns, viel schülerfreundlicher, d.h. es gibt nicht so viele Pflichtfächer und die Kinder können Fächer nach ihren Neigungen wählen. Florian hat überwiegend Werken und Computerunterricht, Lucia hat drei verschiedene Kunstkurse und Textildesign und Felix verbringt die meiste Zeit mit diversen Sportarten.

Im Großen und Ganzen ist es hier so wie wir es uns vorgestellt haben, die Kiwis sind sehr nette und lustige Menschen, Christchurch ist eine schöne Stadt und inzwischen verstehen wir auch den typischen Kiwislang ganz gut, sie ziehen das e und i soooo lang!

Außerdem findet man hier in der Stadt eine große Vielfalt an Einwanderern, echt „Multi-Kulti". Etwas schwer ist es nach wie vor mit den Lebensmitteln, viele unserer Lieblingszutaten gibt es gar nicht oder nur sehr teuer, aber dafür ist das neuseeländische Obst und Gemüse super lecker, vor allem die einheimischen Mandarinen!

Unterschätzt haben wir den Zustand der Straßen. Wir haben keinen Geländewagen gekauft und das schon bitter bereut, weil man für alles, was nicht Hauptverkehrsstraße ist, einen solchen braucht. Unterschätzt haben wir auch den Arbeitsmarkt, es ist zumindest hier in Christchurch nicht leicht, ohne eine anerkannte Ausbildung einen Job zu bekommen.

Völlig überrascht hat uns der enorme Preisanstieg von 4 % in den letzten 6 Monaten. Wir hatten ja die Hoffnung hier mehr Geld zum Leben zu haben als in Berlin, kommen aber gerade so über die Runden im Moment, aber das geht vielen Kiwis so. Ach ja und weit unterschätzt haben wir auch die Schönheit des Landes und des Himmels!

Cheers, Familie Kux

[From: Kabel eins, Mein neues Leben, 2009]

Grammar you can use

► 1.3

Answers:

► p. 172

D Check your grammar 4

1. The present perfect and the simple past

Finish these sentences with the correct forms of the present perfect or simple past.

a We ***arrived*** (arrive) in New Zealand on 26 August last year.
b We ... (live) here now for six months.
c First, we ... (rent) a flat in Auckland, but then we ... (buy) a house in Christchurch.
d Our son and daughter ... (be) pupils at a school here now for three months and they love it.
e How long ... (you / be) a pupil at this school?
f When ... (you / start) learning English?
g What ... (you / do) yesterday evening? - I ... (go) to the cinema.
h My family ... (live) in Germany since the 1980s.

2. Comparison of adjectives

Complete the sentences with the correct forms of the adjectives.

a (beautiful) New Zealand was even ***more beautifu***l than the German family expected.
b (hard) Sometimes families who emigrate find life ... than at home.
c (good) But sometimes, of course, life in the new country is much ... than at home.
d (big, big) New York is ... than London, isn't it? – Yes, but it isn't as ... as Tokyo.
e (cold, cold) What's winter like in your new country? – It's ... Much ... than at home.
f (bad, bad, slow) The only problem here is public transport. It's definitely ... than at home. In fact, I think it's the ... public transport system I've ever experienced. It's certainly the ...

E Increase your wordpower (Negative prefixes)

Negative prefixes are letters that are added to the beginnings of words so that they mean the opposite.

1. Copy and complete the grid. Use your dictionary if necessary.
2. Practise writing sentences with positive and negative words from the grid:
   In life, some things are possible, others are impossible.

dis- im- il- in- ir- un-

possible	*impossible*	realistic	...
regular	...	correct	...
important	...	typical	...
honest	...	polite	...
organised	...	successful	...
friendly	...	credible	...
formal	...	happy	...
legal	...	interesting	...

2 From Africa to Europe (A photodocumentary)

A young African man waits for a bus in a European city. He lives and works here now, but when he first arrived, like thousands of others, he was an 'illegal immigrant'. But what is the young man's story? Why – and how – did he come to Europe? In 2006, a TV documentary used photographs and interviews to show his journey from his home in Africa to start a new life in Europe. You are going to watch parts of the documentary. It is called: *Kingsley's Crossing*.

A Before you begin

1. In a small group, talk about the problem of illegal immigrants. What ideas come into your mind when you hear this expression? Make a list of keywords.
2. The text below will help you to understand the photodocumentary. Read it now and write a class quiz about it.

Northwestern Africa covers an area of around eight million square kilometers, very approximately the same as Europe including Russia. Algeria, the largest country, is around four and a half times the size of Germany.

The geography and climate of the region are extremely varied. The south is predominantly warm and wet, with tropical rain-forests and some savanna. Towards the north, this gives way to the Sahel, arid grasslands with low scrub and scattered trees. To the north again lies the Sahara Desert, a vast, empty sea of sand where temperatures regularly reach 50°C. In the far north, the Atlas mountains separate the desert from a narrow coastal belt where the climate is Mediterranean. Some of the region's most important cities – like Tunis and Algiers – are to be found here along the coast.

Black Africans have lived in the southern part of the region for thousands of years. The first inhabitants of the northern areas were the Berbers, the desert nomads. However, the region has seen many invasions by Arabs in the north and throughout the whole region by Europeans. The French, the Spanish, the British (and briefly the Germans) all colonised Northwestern Africa. Today, French and English are widely spoken as official languages – plus Arabic in the north.

14 *predominantly:* mostly
17 *give way to sth.:* become sth.
17 *arid:* very dry
18 *scrub:* bushes
18 *scattered:* verstreut

Kingsley's Crossing, part 1: Desperate to migrate

B Understanding and analysing

DVD 2

Sound and (moving) images ▶ 1.2

1. (Comprehension) Watch part 1 of the video. Note down the main things you learn about:
   - Kingsley's job,
   - the situation in his country,
   - his family,
   - why he decides to go to Europe,
   - how Kingsley's parents help him to go.
2. (Analysis) Watch again. Copy and complete this grid.

WHAT (HAPPENS)?	EFFECT ON US?
The video shows us how Kingsley and his family live, for example, ...	*This helps us to imagine ...*
We see Kingsley talking to his parents. They ...	*This helps us to understand ...*
At the end, Kingsley and his parents look ...	*This has the effect on us that ...*

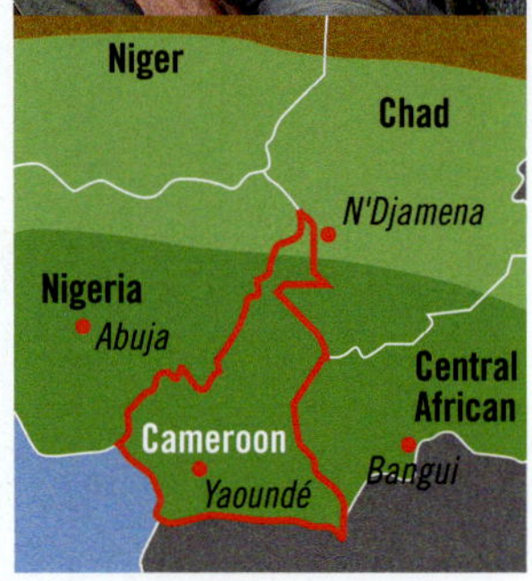

Kingsley's Crossing, part 2: The journey north

CD 3

In this part, you will hear a commentary about his journey from his home in Cameroon to the North African coast. The photos on the next page illustrate this.

C Before you listen

Sound and (moving) images ▶ 2

Look at the photos and speculate about what you will learn in part 2.
- What different landscapes will Kingsley travel through?
- How will the climate affect him?
- What emotions will Kingsley feel at different times? Why?
- What will be the 'best' and 'worst' parts of his journey? Why?

D Understanding and analysing

Sound and (moving) images ▶ 1.2

1. (Comprehension) Listen and take notes about:
   - the main things that happen,
   - Kingsley's emotions at different points on his journey.
2. (Analysis) Explain what effect scenes like those in the photos have and why the documentary included them.

Europe in sight!

The forest of Nador

The ghetto in Rabat

Across the Sahara!

Goodbye Cameroon

Waiting in Agadez

Kingsley's Crossing, part 3: Dangerous Atlantic crossing

DVD 4

After his disappointment in Tangiers, Kingsley has to wait several weeks for another chance to cross to Europe. A new smuggler takes him to El Aaiún. You are going to watch his crossing from there to Europe.

Sound and (moving) images
▶ 2

E Before you watch

1. Where in Europe do you think the smuggler will try to take Kingsley and his friends?
2. Describe Kingsley in the photo on the right. How do you think he is feeling? Why? Speculate about what may happen during the crossing.

F Understanding and analysing

1. (Comprehension) Watch part 3 and take notes under these headings. Then sum up orally what happens:
   - waiting for the crossing
   - the first attempt
   - the crossing
   - at the end
2. (Analysis) Work with a partner or in a small group to collect your ideas about the questions below. Then write a short text about this part.
   - How would you describe the photos in this part of the programme, especially during the crossing itself? Give an example.
   - What is the message the programme makers send to us, the viewers, in this part?

Kingsley's Crossing, part 4: The promised land

Kingsley and his friends are detained by the Spanish authorities in Spain for two weeks. Then finally, they are released. Kingsley is in Europe!

G Before you watch (Creative writing)

Guess how the story will end.

Written texts
▶ 5.2e

1. Work in a small group and collect your ideas about the questions below.
   - Will Kingsley stay in Spain or will he perhaps go to live in another European country? (Tip: he speaks English and French.)
   - Will he be able to become a legal immigrant, get a job etc.?
   - How will he feel about finally being in Europe? Will he stay in Europe long-term?
2. Write the end of the story.

DVD 4

H Understanding and analysing

1. (Comprehension) Here is one of the photographs from part 4. Watch, then use the photo and the prompts below to write a text about this part.
   In this photo Kingsley is feeling ... because ...
   He describes this moment as: ...
   Lots of people helped Kingsley to reach this moment, for example ...
   So do these feelings last for Kingsley? Well, ...
   This happens because ...
   At the very end of the programme, ...

2. (Analysis) Write a short text about this part of the programme. Begin like this:
   In this part of the programme we ...
   The effect is ...

I Talk and write about the complete photodocumentary

Work in small groups on the following tasks.

1. Sum up in a few sentences and as far as possible in your own words:
   - why Kingsley comes to Europe,
   - how he comes,
   - what happens and how he feels once he is here.
2. Characterise Kingsley. What impression of him does the photodocumentary give us? The expressions from the box will help you. Use your dictionary to check the meanings of any words you are not sure of.

(dis)honest • (un)realistic • (un)reliable • brave / courageous • cold-hearted • desperate • determined • egoistic / selfish • emotional • frustrated • grateful for sth. • hard-working • hopeful • lazy • optimistic • pessimistic • be afraid of • be disappointed • be willing to do sth. • do everything for sb. • face danger • give up • have a goal • have good / bad intentions • realise a dream • trust sb.

The documentary	characterises Kingsley as someone gives us the impression that	who is ... Kingsley is ...
Kingsley is portrayed	in the documentary as a person	who ...
The impression that we get	from the documentary is	that ...

3. (Reacting to the text) Think back to the ideas that you had about illegal immigrants before you watched the documentary, and then think how you feel now after watching. Which statement(s) below do you agree with? Give your reasons.
   a I can understand much better now why people like Kingsley come to Europe.
   b I think Europeans should help people like Kingsley much more.
   c I understand that the situation in poor countries is bad, but the answer is not for people like Kingsley to come to Europe - Europeans have their own problems.

[From: Kingsley's Crossing by Olivier Jobard and MediaStorm]

SEQUENCE

02

BECOMING AN ADULT

Adolecence is the time in a person's life between childhood and adulthood. This sequence looks at the issues that adolescents face as they become adults, the decisions they have to make, and some of the highs (and lows) of being a 'teenager'.

Collect ideas

It is said that "a picture is worth a thousand words". The pictures on these two pages illustrate some of the themes that you will talk about in this sequence. But what are the themes? And how do the pictures convey these ideas?

Activity chest
▶ 13

1. Match the pictures and the concepts below, then compare with a partner.

conflict	belonging	the future
decisions	dropping out	

2. Can you suggest alternative themes for any of the pictures?
   I think picture ... could also convey the idea of ...

Sound and (moving) images
▶ 2

3. Explain how the pictures convey the ideas you have discussed. Why do you think of these themes when you look at them?

Picture A (B, C ...)	shows ...	a girl on a road / a ...
The picture / It	gives you / evokes	the impression that ... / the idea that ...
	suggests / implies / illustrates the problem of ...	

Written texts
▶ 5.2a

Written texts
▶ 5.1

4. Work in groups to collect more ideas about the themes. Develop a mindmap and present it to the class.
5. Talk in class. Do you think that the pictures present a negative image of adolescence? (This sequence is not just about 'bad' things.) What ideas about adolescence do you think are missing? Are they more positive?

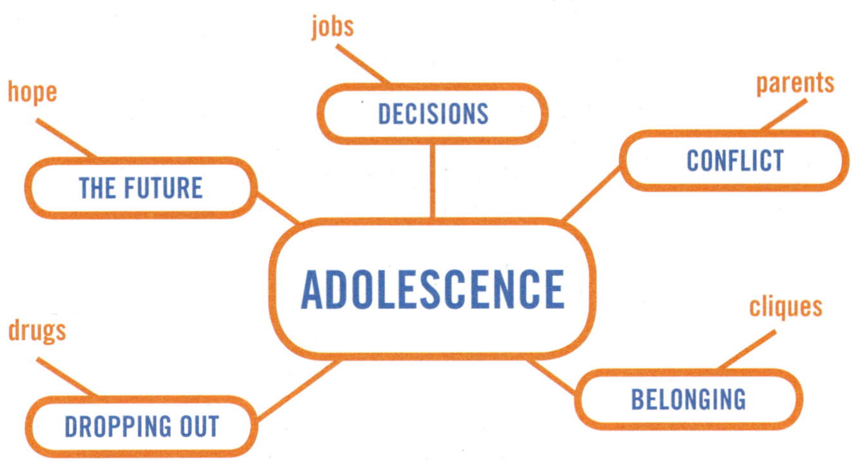

Check your grammar 1 (The simple present)

Grammar you can use
▶ 1.1

Answers
▶ p. 172

1. Facts, situations etc. that are true generally / with adverbs like *sometimes* etc.

a I … (live) in Germany.
b My best friend … (come) from Hungary.
c Adolescence … (be) a difficult time for many people.
d Young people … (often / face) problems in their lives.
e Some … (regularly / have) conflicts with parents or teachers, for example.
f They … (usually / have) to make lots of important decisions, too.
g In many western countries, there … (be) teenagers who … (live) on the streets.

2. To talk and write about texts

a In this text, the writer … (tell) us about her experiences as a teenager.
b It … (say) in the text that growing up … (can) be hard.
c I … (think) that this song … (express) the idea of 'being alone'.
d The poem … (make) it clear that many of the stereotypes that we … (have) about people … (be) simply wrong.
e This movie … (be) a thriller. In it, two men … (arrive) in a strange town. On their first night there, someone … (murder) one of the men. The other man … (travel) across the USA to find the killer. At the end of the movie, there … (be) an exciting car chase in Chicago.

3. Questions

You have to write an interview with a character from a story. Make questions to ask the character.

a "I live in New York." (WHERE?) ***Where do you live?***
b "My parents are from Central America." (WHERE?)
c "My sisters and I hate America because we are poor here." (WHY?)
d "We go back to Central America every summer." (HOW OFTEN?)
e "We visit our relatives there." (WHAT / DO?)
f "About 20 other people from Central America go to my school." (HOW MANY?)

4. Negatives

You have to compare the lives of two people from newspaper articles. Write negative forms of the verbs.

a Person A has an easy life. Person B, however, ***doesn't have*** (have) an easy life.
b Person A lives with his parents. Person B, on the other hand, … (live) at home.
c Person A goes to school every day. In contrast, person B … (go) to school regularly.
d The two people have some things in common. They both live in small towns. They … (live) in a big city.
e They are both in a band. They … (sing), they play instruments.
f Both have problems with girls. They … (get on) well with them.

TOPIC 01

Being yourself

1 'Numb' (A song)

You are going to listen to a song called *Numb* by the American band Linkin Park.

A Before you listen

Sound and (moving) images ▶ 2

1. Look at the picture. How do you think the boy is feeling? Why?
2. Look up the word 'numb' in your dictionary. In what situations might a person feel numb? Give concrete examples. Could the word 'numb' describe the boy in the picture? Why (not)?
3. The Linkin Park song that you are going to hear is called *Numb*. What do you think it may be about?

B Understanding the song

CD 4

Sound and (moving) images ▶ 1

When you listen, concentrate first on 'getting the gist' – getting a general understanding. Then as you listen again, you will find that you begin to understand more and can add details.

1. Listen once. Give your first impression of the song. Find a word to describe it (sad? happy? angry? ...?)
2. 'The song is like a dialogue.' Listen again. Explain what this means. Think about the people in the dialogue and where the dialogue takes place.
3. Listen one more time. The singer tells us in the song that he 'wants' something. Note down what he says then compare your answer with a partner's.
4. Read the song text (the 'lyrics') on the next page. List the reasons the singer gives us for your answer to question 3. Now, using the phrases below, find a theme for the song and sum up what it is about.

The song is about ... / The theme of the song is ...		
In the song,	the singer tells us	that he feels ... For example, ...
The song takes the form of a dialogue with a 'you'. This 'you' could / might be ...		
The singer explains he feels the way he does because ... . Furthermore, ... / Moreover, ...		
Finally, we can conclude that the main message of the song is that the singer wants ...		

Activity chest ▶ 8

✕ **Extra:** Work in a small group. Prepare a 'Freeze-frame tableau' that illustrates the song. One of you is a reporter who can bring the characters to life. Show your tableau to the class.

Numb

VERSE 1

I'm tired of being what you want me to be
Feeling so faithless, lost under the surface,
Don't know what you're expecting of me
Put under the pressure of walking in your shoes
(Caught in the undertow, just caught in the undertow)
Every step that I take is another mistake to you
(Caught in the undertow, just caught in the undertow)

CHORUS

I've become so numb, I can't feel you there
I've become so tired, so much more aware
I'm becoming this, all I want to do,
Is be more like me, and be less like you

VERSE 2

Can't you see that you're smothering me?
Holding too tightly, afraid to lose control?
'Cause everything that you thought I would be,
Has fallen apart right in front of you
(Caught in the undertow, just caught in the undertow)
Every step that I take is another mistake to you
(Caught in the undertow, just caught in the undertow)
And every second I waste is more than I can take

CHORUS

I've become so numb, I can't feel you there
I've become so tired, so much more aware
I'm becoming this, all I want to do,
Is be more like me, and be less like you

BRIDGE

And I know
I may end up failing too,
But I know
You were just like me with someone disappointed in you

CHORUS

I've become so numb, I can't feel you there
I've become so tired, so much more aware
I'm becoming this, all I want to do,
Is be more like me, and be less like you

OUTRO

I've become so numb, I can't feel you there
(I'm tired of being what you want me to be)
I've become so numb, I can't feel you there
(I'm tired of being what you want me to be)

[Words & Music by Chester Bennington, Mike Shinoda, Rob Bourdon, Joseph Hahn, Brad Delson & David Farrell © Copyright 2003]

2 *faithless:* not knowing what to believe in
2 *under the surface:* under water
4 *put sb. under pressure:* force sb. to do sth.
5 *undertow:* Sog, Unterströmung
9 *aware:* noticing what is happening around you
12 *smother sb.:* cover sb. so that they can't breathe
15 *fall apart:* (here) not happen
19 *waste (time):* not to use well the time you have
19 *take sth.:* (here) etwas ertragen
25 *fail:* the opposite of 'succeed'
32 *outro:* conclusion to a piece of music

Written texts
▶ 2.3c

C Analysing the song

We are going to look at two ways in which the song *Numb* puts across its ideas to the listener.

1. The structure of the song

Songs are almost always divided into standard parts – verses, chorus, etc. Look at the structure of *Numb*. (You can see the parts it is divided into next to the lyrics). Explain how the singer uses the structure for certain effects on the listener.

The song *Numb* is divided into	certain standard parts. These are …	
In the verses,	the singer	tells us about … / refers to … / alludes to … / mentions … / describes … / gives us an idea of …
The singer uses the chorus to	emphasise … / focus on … / express …	
By repeating the chorus, the singer	stresses … / underlines … / draws attention to the fact that …	
The lines in the chorus also rhyme.	The rhyme scheme is (abab / aa/bb / …)	
The singer uses this device	to link ideas / to make the lines more dramatic / to make the lines more memorable.	
The song also has an outro.	This repeats … / takes up again the theme of …	
The effect of the outro on the listener is	that the last words we hear are … / that the song finishes with … / that the theme of the song stays in our minds after …	

Written texts
▶ 4.2

2. Imagery

a An example of an image in *Numb* is where the singer tells us that he is "lost under the surface". Thinking of the singer's situation in the song and his feelings, explain this image in your own words:
We learn in the song that the singer feels … (because …)
He compares this feeling to being …
The image conveys to us directly the idea that the singer …
The image helps us to see in our minds / imagine … /
feel just like the singer that …

b Work in groups. Find more images in the song. Draw diagrams or pictures of the images and explain them to the class.

c Write a text to explain how imagery is used to convey the singer's situation and emotions to the listener.

Written texts
▶ 5.1

D Reacting to the song

Talk in class. Comment on whether this song appeals to teenagers. Justify your opinions.

2 Just because … (Poems)

It is not just adults who can be a problem when you are trying to be yourself. Other teenagers (your 'peers') are also often quick to stereotype and criticise you. (You get good grades in your tests, so you are automatically a 'swot'! You live in a certain part of town, so …) The two poems on the next page were written by American high school students.

peer: person of the same age

A Before you read

List some groups of people who are stereotyped at school or by other teenagers generally. Give some of the common stereotypes about these groups.

B Understanding the poems

Activity chest ▶ 5

Working in groups and on projects ▶ 1

1. Look at the first poem. It lists stereotypes about girls. Note down the stereotypes, but use the 'No copying!' rule. Use 'Double circles' to compare your answers in class: *Girls: are not strong / can't act alone / never say what they think / …*
2. Make notes about the questions below, then give a short presentation to your group.
   a Say what you think is the theme of the poem (Tip: think about the writer's attitude to the stereotypes you listed in question 1).
   b Find the phrases in the poems that the writer uses to convey this theme.

✕ **Extra:** When you finish work on the first poem, look at the second in the same way.

C Analysing the poems

Activity chest ▶ 12

Working in groups and on projects ▶ 1

Written texts ▶ 2.3c, 4.2

Work in groups. Use a 'Placemat' to collect ideas about the questions below. Then prepare a short presentation to the class of your ideas.

1. Like songs, many poems also have standard parts. These are usually 'verses' (also called 'stanzas'). Look at the verses in the *Just because* poems:
   a Decide how many different ideas / topics within the main theme each verse contains.
   b Explain the effect this has on the reader.
2. All writers use 'Rhetorical devices' to convey their ideas to their readers. In these poems, for example, the writers use a certain kind of 'repetition'.
   a Identify these repetitions in the poems, and where they come in the stanza.
   b Use the 'Rhetorical devices' section at the back of the book to find the name of this device.
   c Explain the effect the repetition has on the reader.

Just because ...

Just because I'm a girl
I'm not weak
I don't have to depend on
other people
It doesn't mean that I can't voice my
own opinions
or stand up for myself

Just because I'm a girl
I don't cry over boys
I don't plan to major in
home economics
I don't know how
to sew or knit
And trust me, you don't
want to taste my cooking

Just because I'm a girl
I don't have an eating disorder
I don't think that I am fat

Just because I'm a girl
I don't have a subscription to
Seventeen magazine
My room is not pink
I'm not in love with all the boy bands
Brittney Spears is not my idol
And I don't have a Backstreet Boys
poster on my wall

Pegah M.

Just because ...

Just because I live in Kensington
I am not rich
I don't have two Mercedes Benzes
I don't live in a mansion

Just because I live in Kensington
I am not stuck-up
I am not automatically smart
It doesn't mean I can't identify with
others in society

Just because I live in Kensington
I don't have anything given to me
on a silver platter
I don't even own a silver platter
I am not financially secure

Just because I live in Kensington
It doesn't mean I think that I am better
than anyone
Will go farther in life than anyone
Know what I am going to do with my life

Just because I live in Kensington
I don't have more values than you
The values I do have aren't foreign to yours
And I know the value of a dollar

Just because I live in Kensington
Doesn't mean I don't worry
about life day to day
Experience life to the fullest
And I am not ignorant

Just because I live in Kensington

Ari K.

10 *major in sth. (AE):* etwas als Hauptfach studieren
11 *home economics:* Hauswirtschaft
17 *eating disorder:* Essstörung
20 *subscription:* Abonnement
24 *idol:* person you admire and respect
27 *Kensington:* an expensive neighbourhood in San Diego, California
30 *mansion:* big, expensive house
32 *stuck-up:* arrogant
33 *smart (AE):* clever
39 *silver platter:* Silbertablett
47 *values:* ideas about 'right' and 'wrong'
49 *value:* Wert

[K. Ari, M.Pegah / El Cerrito High School, California]

D Reacting to the poems (Creative writing)

Written texts ▶ 5.2e

1. Write your own *Just because* poem. Think of the type of person that you want to be the subject, and collect ideas about common stereotypes about this type of person. Use the structure of the poems you read as a model for your poem.

Activity chest ▶ 11

2. Work in 'Peer review' groups to check and improve your poems. Decide which one poem you would like to present to the class.

3 Role models (A TV documentary)

It often helps you to discover your identity if you can find people whose lives give you ideas – people who can be role models. You are going to watch part of an Australian documentary TV series called *Roadtrip Nation*. In it, three young Australians travel around their country talking to people who have done interesting things in their lives.

The three roadtrippers: (left to right) Bruce Hardy, Kay Lee and Brynn O'Brien, with their camper van nicknamed 'Spud'

A Before you watch

1. Talk about the different sorts of people who are often role models. List some examples.
2. Describe the personal qualities these people have – or the things they have done in their lives – that make them good role models. Give some real-life examples.
3. Say what sort of person you personally admire most. Name someone who would be a good role model for you. Give reasons for your answer.

DVD 6

B Understanding the video

On their roadtrip around Australia, Bruce, Kay and Brynn have reached Melbourne. There, they interview this man, Scott Cupit …

Sound and (moving) images
▶ 1.2

1. Copy the grid below. Watch the video and take notes. Then write a summary of the main points.

- WHAT? / WHERE? Scott's first job
- WHY? His decision to start a new life
- WHAT? Difficulties at first
- HOW? Reasons for succeeding
- WHAT? Scott's advice for others

2. Characterise Scott. Find words to describe his character. Give examples from the video to support your ideas.

Sound and (moving) images
▶ 3

C Analysing the video

1. Explain the filmmakers' intention when they made this video. (Tip: think of non-fictional text types such as 'persuasive', 'informative', …)
2. Now use the grid below to show how the filmmakers use different scenes to put their message across and make the programme clear and interesting for the viewers.

SCENES	THESE SCENES …
Images of Roadtrippers arriving in Scott's studio	*This scene shows the 'setting' for the episode and introduces Scott.*
Scott talking about his life	
'Close-ups' of the roadtrippers listening to Scott	
The dance sequence near the end	
Bruce talking after the interview about his impressions	

D Reacting to the video

Written texts
▶ 5.2d

1. What do you think of Scott Cupit as a role model?
2. Write a review of the programme for a teenage magazine. Mention: where the programme comes from, what it shows, and why young people may (or may not) find it interesting and useful.

[From: www.roadtripnation.com]

TOPIC 02

Growing up between two cultures

How the Garcia Girls Lost Their Accents

(An extract from a novel)

You are going to read an extract from a novel by the Hispanic American writer Julia Alvarez. In the novel, Alvarez writes about the experience of growing up between two cultures – of being a teenager who is part of an ethnic minority.

A Before you read

1. The text below and on the next page gives you some background information about Hispanic Americans. Find a suitable headline for each paragraph and sum up the most important information in each in your own words.

Who are Hispanic Americans?

One of America's best-known Hispanics – Jennifer Lopez ('J-Lo')

It is not unusual in many parts of the United States to walk down a street and to hear people speaking Spanish. The people you are seeing and listening to in this situation are Hispanic Americans ('Hispanics' for short) – Americans who have their origins in a Spanish-speaking country.

Hispanics are America's largest ethnic minority. There are currently around 45 million – 15 per cent of the total population of 300 million. Black Americans come next (12 per cent), then Asian Americans (4.3 per cent). They are also the fastest-growing minority and in the future it is estimated that a very large part of the American population will be Hispanic (and maybe Spanish-speaking).

St Augustine. The Spanish settled here 55 years before the Pilgrim Fathers arrived in New England

So how did today's Hispanic Americans come to the USA? The very first came from Spain itself. In the 16th century, Spain was the world's biggest sea-power. In 1521, it conquered Mexico (still today the world's largest Spanish-speaking country). In 1565, Spanish settlers founded the town of St Augustine, on the east coast of Florida – 55 years before the English Pilgrim Fathers landed farther north in New England! Over the next 200 years, the Spanish moved west as far as California across the whole of what is now the southern USA.

18 *conquer sth.*: take control (of a country) by fighting

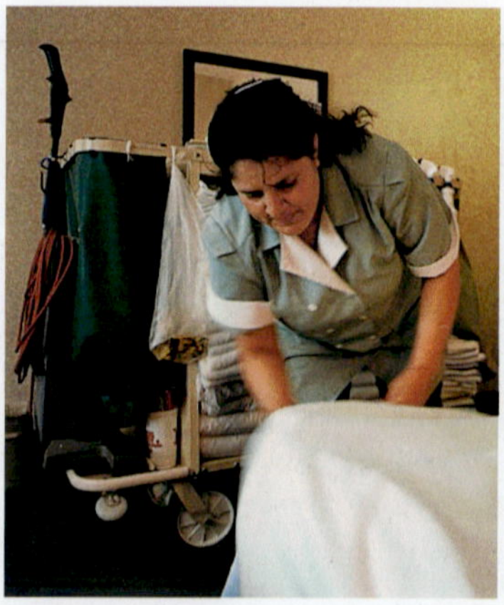

A Hispanic American hotel worker

'The fence' – the U.S.-Mexican border

In the 19th century, however, as the United States grew from the north, Spanish people in the south were pushed out to Mexico, Cuba, the Domican Republic, Puerto Rico, and other countries in Central America. Today, only around 10 per cent of Hispanic Americans are descendants of those first Spanish settlers. The history of modern Hispanic Americans begins with people who came back to the United States from Central America in the 20th century. Because this region is also called Latin America, an alternative name for these Hispanics is 'Latinos'.

Over the last 100 years, millions of Latino people have emigrated from Central America to the United States. Some came because there was political oppression or a revolution in their home country. Most, however, were simply extremely poor and wanted to find a better life. Life for Latino Americans in the United States is certainly better than at home, but for the majority, it is often still hard. Generally speaking, Latinos are among the country's poorest citizens and often have unskilled jobs like cleaners, construction workers or farm workers. Another major problem is that many are not there legally. Today, it is estimated that around nine million of the Hispanics living in the States are illegal immigrants. This problem is so serious, in fact, that in 2005, the U.S. government began building a barrier to stop people crossing into the USA from Mexico. 'The fence' is now over 3,200 kilometers long.

29 *descendant:* son, daughter, grandchild, etc. who comes after earlier members of a family
34 *oppression:* Unterdrückung
38 *unskilled (job):* needing little or no training

2. Collect your ideas in class about growing up between two cultures. Say why some young people find themselves in this situation and describe the difficulties they can face.

Young people can grow up between two cultures	when	their parents / grandparents are from ... they were born in ... (and then came to ...) *(other reasons ...?)*
This situation can sometimes be difficult	because	the young person's life at home ... the young person's life outside their home ... their parents' ideas ... the ideas of people in the country where they live now ... the language / food / habits they are used to at home ... other young people in the country where they now live ... the society generally in which they now live ...

The Dominican Republic

A New York street in the 1960s

How the Garcia Girls Lost Their Accents, part 1

The time is the early 1960s. The Garcia de la Torre family – Mami, Papi, and their four daughters – have just moved from the Dominican Republic to The Bronx district of New York. Back home, Papi was a doctor, an important and wealthy man. However, the Sixties were a dangerous time politically in the Dominican Republic. Papi took part in a plot to overthrow a dictator, there was a revolution … the result was that the family had to leave the island and flee to the United States.

For three-going-on-four years Mami and Papi were on green cards, and the four of us shifted from foot to foot, waiting to go home. Then Papi went down for a trial visit, and a revolution broke out, a minor one, but still.

He came back to New York reciting the Pledge of Allegiance, and saying, "I am given up, Mami! It is no hope for the Island. I will become *un dominican-york.*" So, Papi raised his right hand and swore to defend the Constitution of the United States, and we were here to stay.

You can believe we sisters wailed and paled, whining to go home. We didn't feel we had the best the United States had to offer. We had only second-hand stuff, rental houses in one red-neck Catholic neighborhood after another, clothes at Round Robin, a black and white TV afflicted with wavy lines. Cooped up in those little suburban houses, the rules were as strict as for Island girls, but there was no island to make up the difference. Then a few weird things happened. At school, epithets ("spic", "greaseballs") were hurled our way. Some girlfriend of Sandi's got her to try a Tampax, and Mami found out. Stuff like that, and soon she was writing to preparatory schools (all-girl ones) where we would meet and mix with the "right kind" of Americans.

We ended up at school with the cream of the American crop, the Hoover girl and the Hanes twins and the Scott girls and the Reese kid who got incredible care packages once a week. You wouldn't be so gauche as to ask, "Hey, are you related

1 *going on:* almost
1 *green card:* visa to stay and work the USA
2 *shift:* move
3 *trial visit:* visit to find out about a situation
4 *Pledge of Allegiance:* amerikanischer Treueid
4 *I am given up … dominican-york* = I have given up, Mami! There is no hope for the Island. I will become a Dominican New Yorker.
8 *wail:* cry and shout
8 *pale:* become white
8 *whine:* jammern
10 *red-neck:* poor, uneducated (person)
11 *Round Robin:* American shop where clothes are very cheap
11 *afflicted with sth.:* suffering from sth.
11 *cooped up:* eingepfercht
14 *epithet:* adjective
16 *preparatory school (AE):* private school
18 *cream of the America crop:* children of America's richest people
18 *Hoover:* William Hoover, inventor of the vacuum cleaner
20 *care package:* parcel (of sweets etc.) from home
20 *gauche:* ungeschickt, naiv

21 *attachment:* family relationship
24 *supposition:* idea
27 *filthy rich:* extremely rich
28 *smack of sth.:* nach etwas riechen
29 *pantyhose (AE):* Strumpfhose
29 *candy (AE):* sweets

to the guy who makes vacuum cleaners?" (You could see all those attachments just by the way Madeleine Hoover turned her nose up at you.) Anyhow, we met the right kind of Americans all right, but they didn't exactly mix with us.

We had our own kind of fame, based mostly on the rich girls' supposition and our own silence. Garcia de la Torre didn't mean a thing to them, but those brand-named beauties simply assumed that, like all third-world foreign students in boarding schools, we were filthy rich and related to some dictator or other. Our privilege smacked of evil and mystery whereas theirs came in recognisable pantyhose packages and candy wrappers and vacuum cleaner bags and Kleenex boxes.

Activity chest ▶ 13

B Understanding the text

1. Read the text for a general understanding. Make notes in a diagram like the one below, then compare with a partner and tell the class your ideas ('T-P-S').

SETTING (where and when the action takes place)	CHARACTERS (people we meet in the story)	MAIN EVENTS (what happens)
Bronx, New York ...	*Mami* *Papi* ...	*Family lives in NY "on green cards" (not permanent citizens).* *Papi ...* *After that the family lives in* ...

Working in groups and on projects ▶ 1

2. Now look at the text in more detail. Work in small groups to collect ideas about the following questions, then report to the class.
   a Describe the daughters' feelings about their new home. Contrast their feelings about the States with those about their old home in the Dominican Republic. Give examples from the text to back up your ideas. Finally, find one sentence in the text that you think sums up their feelings well.
   b Outline the reasons why the girls go to a private school after a while. Find the character in the story who is most responsible for this decision and explain why he or she makes the decision.
   c Describe the girls' experiences at the school and characterise them as positive or negative. Give reasons for your point of view.
3. Write a text that summarises your findings for questions 1 and 2.

✕ **Extra:** Work in small groups to look in detail at the characters you meet in this extract.
   a With information from the text, try to form a picture of them and find words to describe them.
   b Choose one character that interests you and, using a scene from the story, prepare a 'Freeze-frame tableau' that brings the character to life.

Activity chest ▶ 8

Written texts
► 2.3a

C Analysing the text

We are going to look at two ways in which Alvarez tells the story and the effect these have on the reader.

1. Narrative perspective

a Say who tells the story – who is the 'narrator'? Explain, with examples from the text, how you know this from the personal pronouns that Alvarez uses.

The story is told by / is told through the eyes of …		
The narrator of the story is …		
We know this / can see this	because	the writer uses the personal pronoun *(he? she? we?)*
For example, …		

b Consider the effect that this type of narrator has on the reader. Think about:
- the person / people in the story you feel 'close to',
- your attitude as a reader towards Mami and Papi,
- your attitude as a reader towards the rich girls at the preparatory school.

This narrative perspective has an effect on the reader in the following ways.	
First, the reader	feels close to / identifies with / shares the feelings of …
This is especially important for teenage readers because …	
Second, the reader also sees characters through the eyes of the narrator and therefore forms certain opinions.	
For example,	we feel that Mami / Papi is …
Another example is the girls at the school.	
Through the eyes of the narrator,	we get the impression that they are …
This is important because the theme of the story is …	

2. Use of language

Sometimes writers don't give us information directly – we have to 'read between the lines'. Look at the extracts below, and explain their meaning in your own words:

a "…the four of us shifted from foot to foot, waiting to go home." (lines 1-2)
This tells us that / implies that … / From this we can deduce that …

b "I am given up, Mami! It is no hope for the Island. I will become *un dominican-york.*" (lines 4-5)

c "…where we would meet and mix with the 'right kind' of Americans." (lines 16-17)

Written texts
► 5.2e

D Reacting to the text (Creative writing)

"Cooped up in those little suburban houses, the rules were as strict as for Island girls, but there was no island to make up the difference." (lines 11-13).
Imagine that you are one of the girls in the story. Using the same narrative perspective as in the original extract, write a text in which you say what life is like for you and your feelings about it.

How the Garcia Girls Lost Their Accents, part 2

But hey, we might be fish out of water, but at least we had escaped the horns of our dilemma to a silver lining, as Mami might say. It was a long train ride up to our prep school in Boston, and there were guys on the train. We learned to forge Mami's signature and went just about everywhere, to dance weekends and football weekends and snow sculpture weekends. We could kiss and get pregnant. We could smoke and no great aunt would smell us and croak. We began to develop a taste for the American teenage good life, and soon, Island was old hat, man. Island was the hair-and-nails crowd, chaperones, and icky boys with all their macho strutting and unbuttoned shirts and hairy chests with gold chains and teensy gold crucifixes. By the end of a couple of years away from home, we had more than adjusted.

And, of course, as soon as we had, Mami and Papi got all worried they were going to lose their girls to America. Things had calmed down on the Island and Papi had started making real money in his office up in the Bronx. The next decision was obvious: we four girls would be sent summers to the Island so we wouldn't lose touch with *la familia*. The hidden agenda was marriage to homeland boys, since everyone knew that once a girl married an American, those grandbabies came out jabbering in English and thinking of the Island as a place to go get a suntan.

The summer plan met with annual resistance from all four of us. We didn't mind a couple of weeks, but a *whole* summer? "Have you got anything better to do?" Mami questioned. Like yes, like *yes* we did, if she and Papi would only let us do it. But working was off limits. (A boss hiring a young girl was after only one thing. Never mind if his name was Hoover.) Summer time was family time. Big time family time, a whole island of family, here a cousin, there a cousin, everywhere we turned a kissing cousin was puckering up at us.

Winters whenever one of us got out of line, Mami and Papi would march out the old "Maybe what you need *right* now is some time back home to help set you straight." We'd shape up pretty quick, or pretend to. Sometimes the parents upped the ante. It wouldn't be just the bad daughter who'd be shipped back, but *all four girls*.

By the time the three oldest were in college – we all started out at the same all-girls one, of course – we had devised as sophisticated and complicated a code and underground system as Papi had when he and his group plotted against the dictator. The parents' habit was to call us on Friday or Saturday nights

3 *escaped the horns of … 'silver lining'*: Mami mixes up two idiomatic expressions: 'horns of a dilemma'= Zwickmühle; silver lining = gute Seite (einer schlechten Situation)
9 *forge sth.*: etwas fälschen
14 *croak:* tell the girls' parents
16 *chaperone:* person who makes sure that boys and girls are not alone together
16 *icky:* eklig, schmierig
16 *strut:* stolzieren
18 *teensy:* tiny, very small
19 *adjust:* learn to live in a new situation
23 *obvious:* clear
24 *hidden agenda:* Hintergedanke
26 *jabber:* plappern
28 *annual:* jährlich
28 *resistance:* Widerstand
28 *not mind sth.*: not be against sth.
31 *off limits:* not allowed
34 *pucker up:* put your lips ready to kiss sb.
35 *get out of line:* do something the parents don't like
37 *shape up:* behave correctly
37 *pretend:* vorgeben
38 *up the ante:* den Einsatz erhöhen
41 *devise sth.*: invent, work out sth.
41 *sophisticated*: clever and refined

around ten right before the switchboard closed. We took turns "on duty" to catch those calls. But Mami and Papi were like *psychic*. They *always* directed the first call to the missing daughter, and when she wasn't in, they'd ask to talk to another missing daughter. The third, on-duty daughter would get the third call, in which the first question would be, "Where are your sisters?" At the library studying or in so-and-so's room getting tutored on her calculus.

At home or in college, we kept most things from the old people, but sometimes they caught on and then we rotated the hot seat.

Fifi was on for smoking in the bathroom. (She always ran the shower, as if smoking were a noisy activity whose hullabaloo she had to drown out.)

Carla was on for experimenting with hair removal cream. (Mami threw a fit, saying that once you got started on that road, there was no stopping – the hairs would grow back thicker, uglier each time. She made it sound like drinking or drugs.)

Yoyo was on for bringing a book into the house, *Our Bodies, Our Selves*. (Mami couldn't quite put her finger on what it was that bothered her about the book. I mean, there were no men in it. The pictures all celebrated women and their bodies, so it wasn't technically about sex as she understood it up to then. But there were women exploring "what their bodies were all about" and a whole chapter on lesbians. Things, Mami said, examining the pictures, to be ashamed of.)

Sandi was on when a visiting aunt and uncle dropped in for a visit at college early Sunday morning. (She wasn't back yet from her Saturday night calculus tutorial.)

It was a regular revolution: constant skirmishes.

[From: How the Garcia Girls Lost Their Accents by Julia Alvarez, Bloomsbury 2004]

44 *switchboard:* Telefonzentrale
49 *get tutored:* have lessons from another student
51 *catch on*: see through a lie
52 *be on (the hot seat)*: be in trouble
54 *throw a fit:* einen Anfall bekommen
65 *drop in:* visit unexpectedly
68 *a regular revolution:* eine echte Revolution
68 *skirmish:* short battle in which no-one is seriously injured

E Understanding the text

1. Work in groups to collect ideas about the questions below.
   a How did the girls feel about America in part 1? How do they feel about it now in part 2?
   b Outline the girls' relationship with their parents in part 2. How do the girls' feelings about things such as how to behave, visiting the Island, working during holidays and getting married contrast with those of Mami and Papi?
2. Now write a text to answer the following question. Check texts with 'Peer review' in your group and choose one text to present to the class. Question: Make clear why and how the daughters' attitude towards the USA changes in part 2 and explain how that affects their relationship with their parents and relatives.

F Analysing the text

Written texts
▶ 4.2

In her writing, Alvarez uses a number of rhetorical devices to convey certain impressions to the reader. We are going to look in detail at two of these: repetition and exaggeration.

Activity chest
▶ 12

1. The major themes of the text are (1) the girls' changed attitude to their old home in the Dominican Republic, and (2) their relationship with their parents. Work in small groups with a 'Placemat'. Look through the text and collect examples of the two rhetorical devices. Decide which of the two themes the examples help us to understand.

DEVICE	EXAMPLE	THEME
Repetition	*"Summer time was family time. Big time family time, a whole island of family, here a cousin, there a cousin, everywhere we turned a kissing cousin was puckering up at us."* …	*attitude to the Dominican Republic*
Exaggeration	*"Island was the hair-and-nails crowd, chaperones, and icky boys with all their macho strutting …"* …	…

2. Explain how the rhetorical devices you looked at in task 1 affect the reader.

The writer uses these rhetorical devices	to convey a particular impression of … / to give us an insight into … / to underline the girls' feelings about …
The repetition of the word(s) / phrase …,	creates the impression that there is 'a lot' (or 'too much') of something – for example, … suggests / indicates / highlights that something is a regular event – for example …
Exaggerated words and phrases such as …	make the story more dramatic / effective / colourful are typical of an American teenager and underline the idea that … have a (slightly) comic effect on the reader – for example, …

Activity chest
▶ 11

3. Write an answer to the question below, then review your texts with 'Peer review'. Analyse how the writer uses certain rhetorical devices to convey to the reader the girls' attitudes to the Dominican Republic and their relationship to their parents.

G Reacting to the whole extract

Written texts
▶ 5.1

Talk in class. Julia Alvarez's aim when she wrote *How the Garcia Sisters Lost Their Accents* was to give an insight into how it feels to grow up between two cultures. How well do you think she succeeded? Give your reasons. If you have personal experience of growing up in an ethnic minority, what did you agree (or disagree) with?

Grammar you can use
▶ 2.1

Answers
▶ p. 172

H Check your grammar 2 (Relative clauses)

Relative clauses are a good way to make the sentences that you write more complex – and so more interesting.

1. Use the relative pronouns in the table to make sentences.

The place	who which / that whose where	lives we learn most about are the girls.
The character		best sums up their attitide is in lines …
The sentence		the girls live are not as big as they would like.
The people in the story		the story takes place is New York.
The houses		families are all rich and famous.
An example		makes this decision is Mami.
There are lots of girls		illustrates this is: "…."

2. Write the two sentences as one, using a relative pronoun.

a There are lots of good examples in the text. They illustrate that the girls now love America. ***There are lots of good examples in the text which / that …***

b The girls make jokes about the young people. These young people live on the Island.

c I think it is wrong to criticise people. These people's lives are just different from ours.

d In the end, the girls come to hate the place. They were born and grew up in this place.

✕ **Extra** Write more sentences of your own with the pronouns.

I Increase your wordpower (Comparing and contrasting)

Use the expressions to finish the sentences. There can be more than one answer.

although - but - however - in contrast - neverthless - on the other hand - while / whereas

a The girls love America … their parents still prefer the Dominican Republic.

b The girls find their new life exciting. …, Mami and Papi think it is 'dangerous' for their daughters.

c The girls don't like their new life at first. …, after a while, they come to love it.

d … the girls' family on the Island think it is right to marry a 'homeboy', the girls themselves find these boys macho and boring.

e The other girls at the private school are from rich families. The Garcia girls … are from a relatively poor family.

f … life in a new country can present lots of opportunities, it can also be very hard – especially at first.

g My family's life was difficult when they first emigrated to Germany. …, they are happy that they live here now.

h Germany can be a wet and cold country. …, many other countries are warm and sunny.

Dream job?

TOPIC 03

Choosing a career is one of the most important decisions that adolescents have to make. Many see this process as finding their 'dream job'.

Collect your ideas

1. Work in small groups. Using your dictionary where necessary, list as many jobs as you can in five minutes. Compare your lists in class.
2. Collect ideas in class with posters.
   a Put up four sheets of paper on your classroom walls with the following headings:

POSTER A
Dream jobs for boys (boys' ideas only!)

POSTER B
Dream jobs for girls (girls' ideas only!)

POSTER C
Dream jobs for boys (girls' ideas only!)

POSTER D
Dream jobs for girls (boys' ideas only!)

   b Boys and girls write their ideas on the posters. On posters C and D, they write what they think are typical dream jobs for the other group.
   c Compare the posters.

Activity chest
▶ 2

3. Now talk in class about what you think makes a dream job. Brainstorm ideas on the board. Choose a student to write them up, then vote for the top reason.

Night on Earth (An episode from a film)

You are going to watch part of a film called *Night on Earth*.

Written texts
▶ 5.2a

A Before you watch

The film is set in Los Angeles. Use this background text to develop a mindmap called 'Hollywood and the film industry'.

The famous Hollywood sign – one of the world's best-known symbols

A cameraman - just one of the people behind the scenes when films are made

Los Angeles, California, is America's second largest city. Known for its smog (there are more cars in the city than people), it is probably most famous as the home of the American movie industry. Hollywood, where all the largest film companies have their studios, is located north-west of downtown LA. Nearby is the district of LA known as Beverly Hills, and it is here that the rich and famous have their luxury homes.

Filmmaking is today a multi-billion dollar industry. The faces in this industry that we most often see are the actors and actresses – some young and unknown, others (the stars) hugely famous and mega-rich. Behind the actors and actresses, however, there is an army of other people who make movies possible. First, there are the scriptwriters. The people who turn the script into a film are the directors. In order to make the film, the director needs a film crew – camerapeople, sound recordists, lighting technicians, make-up artists and many more. Other people in the film industry do jobs that we maybe think about less often. There are those who travel around looking for suitable places ('locations') to make the film. Another important person is the casting agent, whose job it is to find the right actors for the roles in the movie. There is one person or group of people, however, without whom the movie could not be made at all. This is the producer. The producer provides the money for the movie (often several million dollars). It is a big risk: if the movie flops, it can be a financial disaster.

✕ **Extra:** Make a poster that shows who does what in the film industry.

Made in 1991 by the American director Jim Jarmusch, *Night on Earth* consists of five episodes. Each tells a different story set in a different world city. The stories are linked by the facts that they all take place during one night, and in a taxi. The episode you are going to watch is the first episode. It stars Winona Ryder (right) and a popular star of the 1990s, Gena Rowlands.

DVD 7

Activity chest
▶ 13

Sound and (moving) images
▶ 1, 1.2

B Understanding part 1

1. Watch part 1 through once. Don't worry if at first there are parts which are not clear. Concentrate on 'getting the gist' – the main points of the story. Make notes after watching about what you understood, then compare with a partner ('T-P-S').
2. Watch a second time. Collect facts about the two lead characters.

	CORKY	VICTORIA
AGE / PERSONALITY	*young, ...*	
JOB		
SOCIAL STATUS		

3. Compare and contrast the two lead characters at this point in the movie.

At this point in the movie,	the two lead characters seem to be	very similar / different / ...
Corky is ...,	whereas Victoria is ...	

✕ **Extra:** What other things caught your attention while you were watching? For example, did the movie seem rather old to you? Why? What impression did you get of Los Angeles? What did you notice about it? Make notes and tell the class.

Sound and (moving) images
▶ 3.1-3

C Analysing part 1

A movie director uses the camera to tell the story. He/She can't explain to us in words what is happening, but has to show us with moving images. There are two main ways in which the director can do this: with visual details and with different types of 'shots'. We are going to look at how Jarmusch tells his story in this part.

1. Before you begin, look at the information in 'Sound and (moving) images' at the back of the book about different 'camera shots'.
2. Now watch part 1 again and take notes in a grid like the one below. Ask your teacher to pause the film so that you can write your answers.

	DETAIL / SHOT	PURPOSE (WHY?)	EFFECT ON THE AUDIENCE
a	clocks; aerial shots (map); scenes in LA	*'establishing shots'*	*sets the scene / helps the viewer to ...*
b	first shot (close-up) of Corky in her taxi	*introduces a major character*	*our first impression of Corky is ...*
c	men in back of taxi (close-up)	*shows us a typical part of Corky's life*	
d	plane crossing in the background (extreme long shot)		
e	Victoria getting off the plane (long shot)		
f	tracking shot of Victoria walking to the terminal; her body language and facial expressions when she speaks on the phone		
g	director cuts backwards and forwards between Corky's phone call and Victoria's second phone call (medium shots)		
h	Victoria's suitcases arriving while she is on the phone; her body language (medium shot, then long shot)		
i	two women at phone booth; both say "shit" at the same time (two-shot / medium)		
j	Corky almost shuts Victoria's leg in car door; Corky's facial expression after she shuts the door (medium shot)		

3. Now sum up in a text how the director tells his story in this part:
   - *At the beginning of the movie the director needs to set the scene. He does this by ...*
   - *Next, he introduces the two lead characters. His technique here is to ...*
   - *To build up a picture of the characters, Jarmusch ...*
   - *The way he brings the two main characters together is clever. He ...*
   - *He also characterises the relationship between the women. To accomplish this, he ...*

DVD 8

Activity chest
► 13

D Understanding part 2

1. Watch part 2 and again concentrate on understanding the general points. Make notes and compare what you learned with a partner ('T-P-S').
2. Form small groups and watch a second time. Look carefully at the grid below and decide together what important information you need to complete it. Divide up the points in your group and take notes as you watch. Then use the grid to write a more detailed outline of this part of the movie.

Victoria and Corky leave the airport and start driving to Victoria's home in …		
During the journey,	*they begin …*	
After borrowing a phone book from Corky,	*Victoria …*	
In the conversation,	*we learn that …*	
Corky also tells Victoria about her life and her ambitions.		*She says that …*
At the end,	*in another telephone conversation,*	*Victoria …*
From this	*we can guess that …*	

E Analysing part 2

Working in small groups, watch again and analyse how this part of the film conveys its ideas to the audience. Take the following three points into account.

- This part is made up of a mixture shots inside the taxi (two-shots and close-ups, with Corky usually closest to the camera), and shots outside the taxi (usually extreme long shots of the taxi travelling). Explain why the director does this and its effect on the audience.
- The director has to show the emotions of the characters (surprise, happiness, …). Give examples of how he does this visually.
- This whole part is mainly just a conversation inside a taxi. Say what effect this has on the audience.

Sound and (moving) images
► 3.5

Extra: An important aspect of the film is its music. Watch again and make notes about the following points:

- Find words to describe the music Jarmusch uses (amusing? dramatic? …?).
- Where in the extract he uses music.
- How the music at these points adds to the atmosphere of the film / underlines the action / creates a particular effect for the audience.

DVD 9

F Understanding part 3

1. This is the end of the episode. Corky and Victoria arrive at Victoria's house. Before you watch, speculate about how the episode will end.
2. Watch and check your ideas. Sum up in a few sentences what actually happens (use the simple present tense).

G Analysing part 3

Work in small groups again to watch and collect ideas about the techniques that the director uses in this final part. Take the following points into account:

- 'Suspense' is important in movies. Say where in part 3 Jarmusch creates suspense. What about? How?
- When analysing parts 1 and 2, you met some camera techniques like 'close-ups', 'medium shots', 'long shots' and 'extreme long shots'. Look for these shots in part 3. Find some specific examples and explain their effect on the audience.
- Jarmusch ends the episode with a clever device: the telephone in Victoria's bag rings. State briefly what happens, then explain the idea he conveys to us with this device.

H Talking and writing about the whole episode

Collect ideas in class about these questions, then choose one and write a detailed answer.

1. State the theme of the film – what it is about.
2. Remembering that Jim Jarmusch is a Hollywood director, comment on how the film ends. Does it surprise you in any way?
3. Summarise Corky's decision at the end of the episode. List the arguments she uses and compare them with what Victoria offers her. Give your opinion of her decision.
4. Jarmusch said about this film that "... it is made up of things that are usually taken out". In other words, it deals with 'small' events and nothing much happens. Give your reaction to this statement.

Written texts ▶ 5.2d

✕ **Extra:** Write a review of *Night on Earth*. Use 'Peer review' groups to check your texts, then compare reviews in class.

Activity chest ▶ 11

TOPIC
04

When life goes wrong

For some young people, dreams can become nightmares.

Sound and (moving) images
▶ 2

Collect ideas

1. Describe the pictures. What problems do you associate with each scene?
2. How and why do some young people find themselves in the situations you can see?

One reason Another possible reason	why some young people	drink … / take … / become … / get involved in … / feel …	is because …
Some young people …		and that is why they … / so they … / and consequently they ….	

get involved in sth.: in etwas hineingezogen werden
consequently: folglich, als Folge (davon)

3. What sorts of people can help teenagers when they have problems like these? How can they help them?

Teenagers may turn to / ask	teachers / …	for help / support / advice.
A … may help them	by discussing … / suggesting (that) … / recommending(that) … / giving practical help such as …	

1 In (and out of) trouble (Newspaper articles)

The two articles on pages 65 and 66 are from the online edition of a British newspaper. In each, a British teenager tells his or her real-life story.

A Compare the texts

Activity chest ▶ 6

You are going to work in 'Expert groups' to compare the two articles.

1. Work in A and B groups to study the texts. All the A groups study Article 1, all the B groups Article 2. When you study your Article in your group, divide your teenager's story into 'stages'. Find a headline for each stage and note in your own words what happens. Finally, find one stage that you think is particularly important in your teenager's life – a 'turning point' for her or him.

NAME	WHAT HAPPENS
STAGE 1 Headline: *At school*	
STAGE 2 Headline: …	
STAGE …	

Working in groups and on projects ▶ 2

2. Prepare a short talk about your teenager so that you can tell a student from the other group about her / him.
3. Make mixed groups and share information about the two teenagers in the texts.
4. Go back to your 'home' group. Compare your notes to write a summary of the life of the teenager you learned about in step 3.
5. Write a text comparing the lives of the two teenagers.

The two teenagers' experiences are similar in the following ways. Both … There are also differences, however. For example, …		
One of the teenagers	…	but the other … / the other, however, … / on the other hand, …
The turning point for the teenagers was …		This is similar / very different because …
The main difference / similarity between them is (that) …		

B Reacting to the texts

Written texts ▶ 5.1

Talk in class. Agree or disagree with the comments below and add your own.

"These two guys are just stupid and naive!"	"This kind of thing can happen to anyone. It is a matter of luck."	"The stories show that where you grow up can affect your life."
"It is up to parents and schools to make sure young people don't get into trouble."	"These two are OK now, but I don't think they will stay out of trouble! Once a thug always a thug!"	

Written texts ▶ 5.2c

✕ **Extra:** Write a letter to the editor of the newspaper in which you express your views about the stories.

MECHAK BLAKE, 19

❛ I THINK a big part of the problem when I was younger was that I was bored out of my head. The local youth clubs didn't offer anything that appealed more than hanging about on street corners with my mates. I didn't enjoy school and would spend my time hanging around Oldbury, in the West Midlands, where there were plenty of ways you could get into trouble — drink, drugs, street-fighting.

Making music … Mechak

For young males, even if you are just hanging around with your friends, you still get labelled by your postcode and people will have issues with you as a result.

Friends from school are now into drugs or on the dole. That could have happened to me but luckily, when I was 14, I found a youth club that had decks and a mic. I loved DJ-ing and it gave me something to do.

After school I went to college but it wasn't for me and I ended up dropping out. It was at that point I started volunteering full-time at a charity for young people called Krunch in Sandwell. I started running DJ / MC workshops for kids on the verge of being kicked out of school.

The more I did it the more I realised I could get them to talk about things that were bothering them because they came from the same place as me. They seemed to respect me. Kids I have worked with have made demo CDs and are trying to get record deals, which is so rewarding.

I started spending virtually all my time at Krunch and now they pay me for ten hours a week and I volunteer for another ten hours.

I now know my future is in youth work — it has changed my life. In many ways it is a fragile job because you have the lives of these vulnerable young people in your hands.

Politicians are always talking about solving youth crime but it's people like me who can change things.

We need fewer ASBOs and more youth projects. Not all teenagers are thugs.

Just because I wear a hood, it doesn't make me a bad person. ❜

[From: Sun Online, 4th June, 2008]

1 *bored out of my head:* totally bored
2 *appeal:* be interesting
3 *mate:* friend
6 *West Midlands:* region in central England around the city of Birmingham
14 *get labelled (by):* abgestempelt werden (durch)
15 *postcode:* Postleitzahl
16 *issue:* problem
18 *on the dole:* unemployed
19 *deck:* Mischpult
20 *mic:* microphone
21 *college:* (here) berufliche Schule
21 *drop out:* leave before finishing the course
23 *MC = Master of Ceremonies*: Moderator
24 *on the verge of sth.:* very near to sth.
26 *bother sb.:* (here) worry sb.
28 *record deal:* Schallplattenvertrag
28 *rewarding:* lohnend
29 *virtually:* almost
32 *fragile job:* job that can easily go wrong
32 *vulnerable:* verwundbar
36 *ASBO = Antisocial Behaviour Order:* Verwarnung gegen antisoziales Verhalten
36 *thug:* violent person
37 *hood:* Kapuzenpulli

MELETER JAMES, 18

" I WAS always getting into trouble at school.

When I was 14, I had a fight with a girl and one of my teachers said I would end up with a prison sentence if I kept going the way I was.

Meleter … studying law rather than being on the wrong side of it

My mum and dad split up when I was very young. I was living with my dad but when I was 16 I wanted to build a relationship with my mum so I went to live with her. We argued a lot and it didn't work out so I left.

I slept on people's sofas and eventually got a place in a hostel in Peckham, South London. I had no idea about my future and didn't care about myself. I started hanging around with girl gangs who carried knives and guns. People used to say I would end up getting stabbed. Sometimes I think I am lucky to be here.

I was referred to Connexions Direct, an advice service for young people, and they got me a place on a course with the Tomorrow's People charity. I had done courses in hairdressing and music technology but always dropped out. But I felt comfortable at Tomorrow's People. They didn't talk down to you and they listened. I lost four friends to gun crime and could see the problem was getting worse.

So I teamed up with other people on the course to make a DVD for schools about the dangers of carrying guns. We know kids don't listen to older people but we thought they might pay more attention to people like us who know what life is like on the streets. Our message was: "Think before you pick up a gun" and we tried to make it as strong as possible.

In the summer holidays we also ran a football scheme to get the younger kids on one of the housing estates to get up every morning and join in. These are the kids who often get involved in anti-social behaviour because they just hang about.

I've always had a strong drive to survive and pick myself up but now I feel I've given something back. The experience I got on the course helped me get a job at Marks & Spencer and I now have a council flat.

The way my life was going before I started doing community work, I think I would have ended up being on the wrong side of the law. But now I'm applying to study law at college. "

[From: Sun Online, 4th June, 2008]

3 *prison sentence:* Gefängnisstrafe
18 *stab sb.:* jdn. erstechen
19 *refer sb. to sb.:* jdn. an jdn. verweisen
20 *charity:* Wohltätigkeitsorganisation
21 *drop out:* leave before finishing the course
27 *pay attention to sb.:* jdm. aufmerksam zuhören
31 *housing estate:* Wohnsiedlung
34 *pick oneself up:* sich aufraffen
36 *Marks & Spencer:* well-known British department store
36 *council flat:* Sozialwohnung
37 *community work:* work to help people in the local area
38 *end up on the wrong side of the law:* auf die schiefe Bahn geraten
39 *law:* Jura
39 *college:* (here) an institute for higher education

Grammar you can use
▶ 1.8

Answers
▶ p. 172

C Check your grammar 3 (Verbs + infinitive or gerund)

Some verbs are followed by an infinitive (to + verb), others are followed by a gerund (verb + ing), and some can be followed by either an infinitive or a gerund. Give the correct forms of the verbs below.

1. All these verb forms were in the texts about Mechak and Meleter.

a Mechak loved … (DJ).
b After school he started … (volunteer) at a charity for young people.
c He liked it there because the kids seemed … (respect) him.
d Now some of the kids he worked with are trying … (get) record deals.
e Meleter went to live with her mum because she wanted … (build) a relationship with her.

2. These sentences were not in the texts but you could use them when summarising or talking about the texts.

a Mechak didn't enjoy … (go) to school. In fact, he hated … (go) there.
b Mechak enjoyed … (work) at the centre so much that he decided … (get) a job there.
c Mechak plans … (work) with young people in the future.
d Meleter hoped … (build) a relationship with her mum, but it didn't work out.
e She couldn't afford … (rent) a flat, so she slept on friends' sofas.
f Young people often refuse … (listen) to older people, so Meleter made a DVD for them about gun crime.
g After her course at Tomorrow's People, Meleter managed … (get) a job at Marks & Spencer.
h Meleter has learned … (build) a new life for herself. Now, she hopes … (become) a lawyer one day. She certainly doesn't miss … (sleep) on other people's sofas and … (be) involved in gun crime.

D Increase your wordpower (Expressing opinions)

You are taking part in a class discussion. Use the phrases in the box to write sentences about the topics below, then compare with a partner.

- (Personally), I think that …
- As far as I can see, … / It seems to me that … / In my opinion, … / To my mind, … / I'm convinced that …
- I don't think that …
- I'm not so sure that … / I'm not convinced that … / That's wrong! I (don't) think that … / No way! In my opinion, …

a Mechak was pretty stupid when he was at school.
b Meleter was very lucky to find Tomorrow's People and to be able to change her life.
c When young people get into trouble, it is often their parents' fault.
d Teenagers who wear hoods are all bad people.
e Young people often get into trouble because there is nothing to do in the town where they live.
f Being in a gang and getting into trouble is sometimes a normal part of growing up.
g ASBOs are a waste of time.

2 Needing Love (A 10-minute play)

Drama provides a way to explore themes that may be difficult to talk about in everyday life. The play that follows is about one of the most difficult issues of all – attempted suicide. It was written for American high school students.

American high school students rehearse a play in their drama class

A Before you read

People have to feel very desperate before they think of suicide. Suggest situations and events in their lives which could make them feel like this.

Needing Love

The action occurs in the Dombrowski's living room. **Dad** *has just returned from an overnight trip. After a few moments,* **Kathleen** *enters.*

Dad Hi, honey.

Kathleen Dad, I need to talk to you.

Dad What is it?

Kathleen Bonnie ODed on drugs last night.

Dad What?

Kathleen She's in the hospital, in intensive care.

Dad *(Sitting down)* What happened?

Kathleen That's the thing. She took Grandpa's pills.

Dad What do you mean? What pills?

Kathleen His Fiorinal.

Dad I knew he couldn't find them. But that was a couple of weeks ago.

Kathleen She'd been planning this for a long time.

Dad Why?

Kathleen Because of Jeff. You know how she is about Jeff. She's completely crazy when it comes to him. She keeps calling him and taking the bus to his house. He doesn't want anything to do with her.

Dad How is she? Do you know?

Kathleen Not very good. She took quite a few of the Fiorinal pills and some Tylenols too.

Dad How did you find this out?

Kathleen She was over here.

Dad You better start at the beginning.

Kathleen She came over and said she wanted to lie down on my bed. I said OK. I didn't think anything about it. You know she and her dad always fight. I thought she just wanted to get away.

Dad She'd already taken the pills?

Kathleen Yes. She was here a couple of hours, and Liz went in to get her up. Bonnie acted all dumb.

Dad What do you mean?

4 *OD on sth.:* take an overdose (OD) of sth.
28 *dumb (AE):* stupid

Kathleen	Like she couldn't talk right, and she kept falling into the wall. And then she vomited all over my bed. We got her up and took her to the bathroom. After we went back to the living room we heard a thump. We went to the bathroom and found her on the floor, almost unconscious.
Dad	Did you call her father?
Kathleen	She didn't want to see him. She said she just wanted Jeff. If she couldn't have him, she didn't want anything. She just went on and on about how she loved him.
Dad	So what happened?
Kathleen	Liz and I took Bonnie home, and her dad put her to bed. We had to take her home. We didn't know what else to do.
Dad	Didn't he take her to a hospital or call an ambulance?
Kathleen	No. He said he thought she'd be OK.
Dad	Couldn't he see the state she was in?
Kathleen	I guess not. I don't know. Anyhow, she started having convulsions. Then he called for an ambulance. They came and took her to Memorial.
Dad	Poor kid.
Kathleen	It's her own fault. I tried to tell her to forget about Jeff.
Dad	Don't be hard on her, Kathleen. Maybe her home life is bad. She might have needed someone to turn to. Maybe this was just her way of asking for help.
Kathleen	I don't know. She left a note but made sure it wouldn't be found straight away.
Dad	How do you know that?
Kathleen	It was in a folder under her purse. I guess she figured no one would look there right away. *(Shrugs)* She said she needed someone to love her. And if no one did, she wanted to die. She wrote what she'd taken, and how many of each kind. The last sentence just trails off, like she was too tired or too far gone on the pills to finish. I certainly hope she'll be OK. As soon as she's better physically, they're sending her to Mesa Verde, a psychiatric hospital south of town.

31 *vomit:* sich erbrechen
32 *thump:* the sound sb. makes when they fall heavily
34 *unconscious:* ohnmächtig
44 *the state she was in:* how ill she was
45 *convulsions:* Krämpfe
47 *Memorial* = Memorial Hospital
56 *folder:* Ordner, Mappe
56 *purse (AE)* = handbag
56 *figure:* think
57 *shrug (your shoulders):* mit den Achseln zucken
59 *trail off:* stop without a clear ending

[From: *Acting It Out* by M. Cassedy and J. Sturkie, © Resource Publications Inc, 1990]

B Understanding the text

1. List the people you see or hear about in the play and collect factual information about each one. (Tip: there is one of the characters that you may have to guess about.)

KATHLEEN	*The main person in the play. Bonnie's friend. A high school student.*
DAD	*Kathleen's father.*
BONNIE	...
...	...

2. Work in groups to collect information about the main characters and their relationships, giving examples from the text. 'Read between the lines' when necessary.

	CHARACTER	EXAMPLE(S)
KATHLEEN	*- has good relationship with Dad* *- Bonnie's best(?) friend* *- thinks Bonnie's relationship with Jeff is wrong* ...	*- tells him straight away about problem with Bonnie (trusts him)* *- K knows Bonnie very well / Bonnie comes to K's house when she has a problem* *- "You know she's completely crazy when it comes to him." / ...* ...
DAD	...	...

3. With examples from the text again, collect ideas about the questions below then compare answers in class.
   a Characterise Kathleen's role in the play.
   b Decide whether Bonnie's suicide attempt is serious. (Does she really want to die?) Give your reasons. Take into account particularly lines 53 – 60.
   c Explain the reasons behind Bonnie's suicide attempt. Take into account Jeff, Bonnie's father, and the title of the play.

C Analysing the text

Written texts ▶ 2.3b

Collect ideas in a copy of the grid below. Then use the phrases to write a text analysing the play.

AIM OF THE PLAY?	
HOW?	*The suicide is seen through the eyes of ... / told in the words of ...* *'Dad' often asks questions which ...*
EFFECT ON AUDIENCE?	*The play is short, but it can lead to ... / help us to ...* *Because the play is about a young person ...* *Because we hear about the events from a young person, we ...*

The aim of the play is / The play sets out	to explore the idea of ... / encourage people to think about ...
The play takes the form of	a dialogue between ... / a scene in which we see ...
Bonnie's suicide is presented / The story of Bonnie's suicide is told / We learn about the characters / Bonnie's feelings	through the the words of ...
The effect on the audience	is that ...
By watching the play,	the audience can ...

D Further work

Work in pairs or small groups to stage the play *Needing Love*.

Written texts ▶ 5.2e

✖ **Extra:** Look back at some of the situations involving teenagers you have learned about in this sequence. Write your own short play about the topic to encourage discussion.

3 Pubertät ist klasse! (Mediation)

So is being a teenager all 'doom and gloom'? You find this article in a German teenage magazine and would like to use the ideas from it while chatting online to a British friend.

Hat die verflixte Pubertät eigentlich auch irgendwelche Vorteile? Klar! Neben all den Problemen hat die Pubertät durchaus auch ihre guten Seiten, nämlich:

Du bekommst mit den Jahren immer mehr Rechte (wählen gehen, Alkohol kaufen).
Du darfst länger aufbleiben.
Du wirst größer und kräftiger.
Du wirst selbstständig.
Du darfst endlich Filme an 16 oder 18 Jahren anschauen, vorausgesetzt, du hast dieses Alter erreicht ...
Du triffst wichtige Entscheidungen (Schullaufbahn, Beruf ...).
Du wirst größer und körperlich erwachsen (und damit bald auch anders behandelt ...).
Du bringst im Sport bessere Leistungen.
Du sammelst neue Erfahrungen (mit deinem Körper, in der Liebe, im Umgang mit Erwachsenen...).
Du darfst allein auf Partys gehen.
Du kannst einen Freund bzw. eine Freundin haben.
Du bekommst mehr Taschengeld .
Du darfst dein Taschengeld durch Jobben aufbessern.
Du bekommst mehr Respekt.
Du darfst jetzt eher ohne Eltern verreisen.
Du fühlst dich erwachsener.
Du darfst Mofa, Moped, Auto fahren.
Du reichst immer mehr an die Erwachsenen heran.
Du entwickelst in deinem Auftreten mehr Sicherheit.
Du kannst deine Meinung besser mit Argumenten vertreten.
Deine Freiheit wird zunehmend größer.
Du hast es bald geschafft ...

[From: Anja Gerstberger, Juppidu Magazin 2008]

SEQUENCE

03

UNDERSTANDING NEWS AND THE MEDIA

TV, newspapers, the internet and other media play a vital role in all our lives. In this sequence we look at how they provide us with news and how new media technologies are changing the world in which we live.

Collect ideas

1. Look at the dictionary definitions at the top of the next page. List as many differences as you can between the *(mass) media* and the *new media*.
2. Describe the pictures on these two pages. Say which type of media each relates to and what is happening in each. The terms and explanations in the box below will help you.

Sound and (moving) images ▶ 2

- produce / print newspapers / a newspaper printing press
- a TV news programme / a TV studio / a TV news presenter / a cameraman
- a 'citizen journalist' (someone who reports news and interesting events, often with photos or video, on social networking sites like Twitter and YouTube)
- a laptop / portable music player (MP3 player) / headphones
- use a computer / chat / surf (the web) / keep in touch with friends / listen to music …
- mobile phone (AE: cell phone) / text message / threat / (cyber)bullying

the (mass) media /ˈmiːdiə/ noun [+ singular or plural verb] newspapers, magazines, TV and radio considered as a group: *This topic has been discussed a lot in the media. The mass media is / are an important influence on modern society.*

the new media noun [+ plural verb] new information and entertainment technologies such as the internet and mobile telephones: *The new media are changing the way we see the world.*

3. Prepare and give a short talk on the media using the ideas from these pages and the words and phrases below.

The term 'the media' refers to the different ways in which	we get / obtain / receive	information / entertainment.
Traditionally, these ways	included / were	newspapers / …
These are still often called the …	because …	
In the last 20 years, however,	'new' media have emerged / appeared / evolved / come into being.	
These include …		
The new media have dramatically / radically	changed / altered / transformed the world we live in. For example, …	
Using new technology, news and interesting events can also be reported by … on websites such as …		
New technology can have its disadvantages / downside, however. For example …		

emerge: entstehen
evolve: sich entwickeln

✕ **Extra:** Write your personal 'media diary' for the last five days listing what media you used, what for and for how long. Compare your diaries in class.

TOPIC

01

Here is the news

1 What is news? (News stories)

News. There is a huge amount of it every day – in newspapers, online, on TV, even on mobile phones. Here are a few examples of news stories from newspapers and magazines.

A Before you read

Talk in class. Say what news stories have interested you in the last week. Explain why you found them interesting.

Written texts
▶ 2.2e, 3.1

B Understanding the texts

News is often divided into 'news categories'. Skim the stories on these pages and decide which category each story belongs in. Explain your answers and give the main points of each story.

News categories
business – entertainment – politics – science – sport – human interest - technology and the internet

STORY A: This belongs in the category of … Briefly, teenagers were asked to vote for the 'coolest celebrities'. They chose …

✕ **Extra:** Choose one of the stories. Speculate about other information it could contain. Invent details yourself if necessary.

Baby unhurt after falling in front of train

A baby in Australia escaped miraculously unhurt when its stroller fell in front of a moving train.

The mother, who was waiting for a train at Perth railway station, let go of the stroller for an instant and it rolled off the platform on to the railway track.

Despite being carried 40 yards by the train, the 5-month-old suffered only a bump to the head.

A

War on terrorism could last years

James Burnett, Lisbon

Western political leaders warned yesterday that the fight against international terrorism would not be quick or easy.

Meeting at the G8 summit in Lisbon, heads of state of three major EU countries declared that finding solutions to worldwide terrorism "could last for years".

B

Shock polar ice caps warning

A new report has found that the ice at both the North and South Poles is melting faster than previously believed. The report, written by the European Polar Survey Team, raises new fears about the pace of global warming.

C

Telescope finds new world

A telescope that searches space for Earth-like planets where humans could survive has discovered a new world orbiting a star outside our own solar system.

D

McDonald's global sales rise

McDonald's, the world's largest fast food retailer, announced yesterday that its global sales for the year rose by 2.2 per cent. It also plans to open 1,000 new restaurants in Europe this year.

E

Chat room dangers

Research highlights the dangers of online chat rooms for teenagers

Researchers at the University of Boston found that six per cent of the young people they interviewed had arranged to meet a stranger offline.

F

X Factor's Cheryl Cole teenagers' "coolest celebrity"

X Factor judge Cheryl Cole and High School Musical actor Zac Efron have been voted the coolest celebrities among teenagers.

G

Top German footballer to move to Britain

Star German Bundesliga player signs surprise contract with Manchester United

H

"News is what we need to know or what we want to know."

Activity chest
▶ 5

C Talking about the texts

Journalists define news as 'what we need to know or what we want to know'.

1. Which of the stories on the previous two pages would you personally 'want' to read and which do you think you 'need' to read? Give your reasons. Now use 'Double circles' to compare your ideas with those of several partners.
2. Talk in class. How different were your choices from those of other students? Did you agree or disagree about how to classify the stories as 'need to know' or 'want to know'? What reasons were given for how to classify them?
3. Now think about what makes news 'important' or just 'interesting'. In the society in which you live, what sorts of issues do you think everyone should be well-informed about? Why? What sorts of issues are people often very interested in, even if they are not so important? Why? Can some stories be just 'silly' (trivial)? Give examples. Should newspapers report such stories in your opinion? Why (not)?

We need to know about …		
certain events / situations / new developments	because	they affect / concern / are of interest to large numbers of people / we should be informed about … / be aware of … / the information helps us to have / to form opinions about …
We just like reading / hearing about …		
some news stories	because	they are dramatic / amazing / lighthearted / amusing / they have a lot of 'human interest' / they appeal to / interest / fascinate readers who …
I agree / disagree	that some unimportant stories are too trivial / shouldn't appear in newspapers or on TV because …	

Grammar you can use
▶ 4

Answers
▶ p. 172

D Check your grammar 1 (Singular and plural nouns)

The following sentences could all be used when talking about news and the media or about news stories generally. Choose the correct forms of the verbs. Sometimes both are possible.

a Here ***is / are*** the news.
b There ***is / are*** a lot of information on the internet that ***isn't / aren't*** correct.
c The media ***is / are*** one of the most important influences on modern society.
d Politics ***is / are*** an important news topic.
e Sometimes the progress that scientists are making in new technology ***is / are*** amazing.
f The United States often ***lead / leads*** the world with new developments.
g That ***is / are*** good advice.
h The government ***want / wants*** to change the law.
i The police ***is looking for / are looking for*** a criminal who escaped from prison.

2 Fact or opinion? (Three newspaper articles)

You are going to look at three newspaper articles which all deal with one news story: people who have come to Europe as asylum seekers and who live in camps near Calais.

A Before you read

The following text provides background information to the story. Work in pairs. One of you is a reporter, the other an expert on the facts in the text. Prepare an interview to act out for the class.

Asylum seekers in Calais

'The jungle': the camp built by asylum seekers in woods on the outskirts of Calais

Asylum seekers watch as the jungle camp is demolished by French police

Every year, thousands of people from around the world come to Europe to escape from wars at home – in Afghanistan, for example - or to look for a better standard of living. In both cases, they hope that they will be allowed to stay: that they will be given asylum in a European country.

Many migrants end up in France, and a number aim eventually to cross the Channel to Britain because they speak English or just believe that Britain – like Germany – is a liberal country where they will feel accepted. This means that they collect near Calais, a port on the northern French coast, from where it is easiest to reach Britain.

The problem is that under EU laws, it is the country in which they first arrive (France) which must first grant them (or refuse them) asylum. Crossing to Britain is, in fact, illegal (although many try and are usually sent back). However, it can take a long time for the French authorities to look at every case and make a decision. The result is that hundreds of migrants are stranded at the port.

At first, the Red Cross provided a camp for the migrants in the small town of Sangatte (near Calais). In 2002, however, the camp was closed in the hope that people would leave the area. The migrants did not leave. Instead, they built their own makeshift camp, nicknamed 'the jungle', on the outskirts of Calais. Around 1,000 people lived here, including whole families with children. The camp consisted mainly of tents, and living conditions were squalid.

In 2009, French police raided and closed the 'jungle' camp. Plans to build a new Red Cross centre at Sangatte (dubbed 'Sangatte II') were considered, but later dropped.

11 *eventually:* letztendlich
25 *authorities:* official organisations (police, government etc.)
27 *be stranded:* festsitzen
30 *makeshift:* provisional, temporary
31 *nickname sb./sth.:* jdm./etwas einen Spitznamen geben
31 *outskirts:* Vorort, Stadtrand
33 *squalid:* dirty and unhealthy
34 *raid sth:* eine Razzia durchführen in etwas
35 *dub sb./sth.:* give a name to sb./sth.

Article 1: A newspaper news article

The following article is from a British quality newspaper, *The Independent*.

French police move on 'jungle' migrant camp

By Jerome Taylor and Robert Verkaik

Hundreds of Afghan and Iraqi migrants who have been living in squalid conditions on the outskirts of Calais fled their tarpaulin homes today in an attempt to avoid being rounded up by armed police in an anticipated raid tomorrow.

Following pressure from the UK, the French government has vowed to destroy the camp – known locally as "the jungle" – to discourage traffickers and would-be migrants from using Calais as the main staging area to smuggle people on board lorries headed across the Channel.

But the announcement last week by immigration minister Eric Besson that the jungle would be dismantled within days gave the camp's occupants ample opportunity to leave the area.

Charity workers who regularly administer medical aid and food to the thousands of so-called 'sans papiers' (without papers) that flock to the Calais area every year say those inside the camp are determined not to be caught by the crackdown. Some have even gone as far as burning their hands in order not to be identified by their fingerprints. [...]

Home Secretary Alan Johnston yesterday said he was "delighted" to hear that France was closing the camp. He added: "Both countries are committed to helping individuals who are genuine refugees, who should apply for protection in the first safe country that they reach." [...]

The jungle to the east of Calais town centre, close to where many of the lorries stop before boarding onto ferries, has been the main gathering point for Afghans, Iraqis and a small contingent of Iranians. A number of squats closer into town have been taken over by east Africans, mainly Eritreans, Ethiopians and Sudanese. Most refuse to claim asylum in France because the UK is their ultimate goal.

While the French government, including Calais' town mayor, Mme Delannoy, are determined to crack down on the migrants, critics say removing the jungle will simply force the refugees to set up camps further away from the town.

Mme Delannoy added: "This will solve absolutely nothing. Eventually the migrants will return to the area because England will always be 45 km from Calais."

[From: The Independent, 21 September 2009]

4 *tarpaulin:* Zeltplane
5 *round up sb.:* arrest sb.
6 *anticipate sth.:* expect that sth. will happen
9 *vow:* promise
11 *trafficker:* person who helps migrants to move illegally to a country
12 *would-be:* wanting to be
13 *staging area:* Sammelpunkt
18 *dismantle sth.:* take sth. down
19 *occupant:* Besetzer/in
20 *ample opportunity:* plenty of time/chance
24 *flock:* come in large numbers
27 *crackdown:* raid
31 Home Secretary: Innenminister
34 *be committed to sth.:* sich zu etwas verpflichtet haben
36 *genuine:* real
42 *gathering point:* Sammelpunkt
43 *contingent:* group
45 *squat:* besetztes Haus, Gebäude
49 *ultimate:* final

B Understanding the news article

1. Describe the plans that the French government has with regard to the 'jungle' migrant camp, saying when and why they want to carry out these plans.

The French government	plans / intends to …	
This	will happen / will occur / will take place …	
The government has	a number of reasons for	its plans / decision.
First / Second(ly) / Third (ly) …		
This is important	to the French government because …	

2. Sum up the different reactions to the French government's plans that are mentioned in the article.

The reactions of … are given in this article.	
The people living in the camp, who are mainly …, fled … because they … Some even … because …	
The British Home Secretary …	
Critics of the plans, such as …	maintain / claim / say / point out, however, that …
Summing up these findings you can say that	both positive and negative reactions are given / presented.

Working in groups and on projects
▶ 1

Written texts
▶ 2.2e

C Analysing the news article

Work in groups to complete the tasks below. Then report your ideas to the class. Every person in your group should be able to make the report.

1. Talk in your group and sum up what you as a reader expect from a news article. Then say what the intentions of the writers of this article are.
2. Analyse by what means the two writers try to achieve their goal.

ASPECT	METHOD (+ EXAMPLES)	EFFECT ON READER
What we are told about the French government's plans	(facts? the writers opinions? …?)	…
People quoted in the article	(in their own words? 'for' and 'against'? …?)	…
Background information	(given? where? how?)	…
Tone and language used	(dramatic? matter-of-fact? …? complex / simple sentences?)	…
Structure of the article	(headlines etc.? order in which things are presented? …?)	…

Written texts
▶ 5.2c

D Reacting to the news article

Write a letter to the editor of *The Independent* newspaper in which you express your opinion about the closure of the 'jungle' camp.

Article 2: A newspaper leading article

The following article is from the same British quality newspaper, *The Independent*. It appeared the day after Article 1.

Leading article: Europe needs to face up to the migration challenge

Governments cannot go on washing their hands of the problem

First the riot police went in, then the bulldozers. By the time their work was done, the makeshift migrant camp on the outskirts of Calais had been wiped away. Politicians on both sides of the Channel expressed their conviction yesterday that this will help solve the migrant problem that has plagued the French port for almost a decade. If only it were that simple.

The reality is that we have been here before. In 2002, the French government ordered the closure of the Red Cross refugee centre in nearby Sangatte. The authorities argued that this would deter migrants from travelling to the area. It did not. The migrants still came. And in the absence of the accommodation centre, they simply built shanty homes in the countryside. There is every reason to believe the same will happen again. Yesterday's raid was broadcast in advance. Many migrants fled before the police moved in. Most expect those who escaped the net will simply establish a new squatter camp in another location.

The 'jungle' in Calais, as it became known, was certainly a disgrace. An unsanitary eyesore, its existence was unfair to both its inhabitants and the local community. But simply tearing it down does not represent a credible way forward. A more thoughtful strategic approach is required.

First, politicians should look to where the migrants in this area originate. Most are from troubled states such as Afghanistan, Iraq and Sudan. If governments want to get to the root causes of the migration problem, rather than simply treating the symptoms, they should be making greater efforts to stabilise those nations and reduce the incentives for their populations to seek a better life elsewhere. Second, our leaders need to dispense with the fantasy that it is within their power to control migration flows. Some people from poor countries will always want to escape poverty or persecution, and they will endure extraordinary risks and hardship to do so. Furthermore, modern transportation and the open borders of Europe make it impossible to shut them out entirely. [...]

At present many governments are washing their hands of the problem, discouraging asylum seekers from making claims in their own nations and waving economic refugees on their way to Britain, which, traditionally, has been somewhere they can easily find work. [...] Europe urgently needs to face up to the challenge of migration and work together to manage its consequences. Demolishing squatter camps and turning back boats of desperate people are not policies, but displacement activities – and morally bankrupt at that.

[From: The Independent, 23 September 2009]

Headline *face up to sth.:* sich eine Sache stellen
1 *riot police:* Bereitschaftspolizei
2 *wipe away sth.:* make sth. disappear
3 *conviction:* belief
4 *plague sb.:* be a problem for sb.
8 *deter sb. (from sth.):* jdn. von etwas abhalten
9 *in the absence of sth.:* when sth. is not there
10 *shanty homes:* slum houses
13 *location:* place
14 *disgrace:* Schande
14 *unsanitary eyesore*: ungesunder Schandfleck
16 *tear down sth:* destroy sth.
16 *credible:* believable
20 *root cause:* eigentliche Ursache
22 *incentive:* Anreiz
23 *dispense with sth:* auf etwas verzichten
24 *migration flows:* movements of migrants
25 *endure sth.:* etwas ertragen
28 *discourage sb. from doing sth:* jdm. von etwas abraten
29 *wave sb. on their way:* allow sb. to go
34 *displacement activity:* Verschiebung, Vertreibung
34 *bankrupt:* bankrott
34 *at that:* noch dazu

E Understanding the leading article

Point out the main event the writer of the article writes about and sum up his / her opinion of the measures suggested. Include the reasons put forward by the writer for this opinion and any alternative measures that are suggested.

In this article the writer	writes about / considers / examines / reflects on / deals with …
He / She points out that the British and French governments …	
However, the writer	doubts / rejects this / is not convinced of this / is far from sure that this is true / is sceptical of this.
To support / back up this view	the writer mentions / states that / draws attention to the fact that / highlights the fact that / argues that / challenges the idea that …
He / She adds that / goes on to say that / also suggests that …	
In the writer's opinion,	a much better solution would be … / political leaders should instead … / Europe must, in fact, …

Written texts
▶ 2.1, 2.2f

F Analysing the leading article

1. Talk in class. Leading articles appear daily on a special inside page of almost all newspapers. Using this article as an example, define what a leading article is and contrast it with a news article. Decide which of the four main text types a leading article is and why.
2. Work through the tasks below, then compare your answers with a partner's.

   The overall structure of the article

   The article can be divided into four main parts: (1) the headline and smaller headline below it (the 'strapline'), (2) the first paragraph, (3) the long middle section, and (4) the final paragraph.

   a Identify the purpose of each part and explain its effect on the reader. Sum up why the writer has chosen this overall structure for the article.

   Putting forward arguments

   There are a number of different ways in which the writer could write this article. For example, the writer can simply state an opinion. Alternatively, he / she could look at other people's opinions or actions and try to show that they are wrong – and that there may be a better solution.

   b Examine what technique(s) this writer uses. Find specific examples in the text.
3. Prepare a short talk about the article. Your theme is: 'Explain how the writer of this article presents her / his point of view to the reader.'

G Reacting to the leading article

Talk in class. Comment on the article's point of view. Do its arguments convince you? Are the writer's ideas practical and realistic, or vague?

Written texts
▶ 5.2e

✕ **Extra:** Write a different leading article about the closure of the 'jungle' camp. Imagine that you have a completely different viewpoint – for example, that you want to put across strongly the feelings of the French people who live in Calais.

Article 3: A newspaper news article

This is another news article. It is from the online edition of a British tabloid newspaper, *The Sun*, and reports a Christmas party organised for asylum seekers in the 'jungle' camp.

Oh come all ye asylum seekers

BY DAVID WILLETTS in Calais

Meal's a cracker ... asylum seeker scoffs his free dinner (Steve Finn)

HUNDREDS of asylum seekers trying to sneak into Britain were treated to a free Christmas party in Calais yesterday.

Five hundred people - mainly Muslims - got food, drink, gifts and party bags. There were no carols in case they were offended.

A volunteer worker said: "There are not many lorries at the port for them to get on at Christmas. Many will be sleeping rough so this party was to try and make them feel happy."

Meanwhile a new immigrant centre - dubbed Sangatte II - was opened yards from the town's ferry terminal.

The camp, for up to 500 people, was created in defiance of the agreement between Britain and France in 2002 that led to Sangatte's closure. The original centre attracted 67,000 immigrants within three years trying to get to Britain.

Clowns

Yesterday's party at Minck civic hall was organised by local charities C'SUR and Belle Etoile. Entertainers included a clown dressed as Santa and local children singing Ethiopia's national anthem.

Pasta, chicken and cake were served instead of traditional turkey dinners.

A C'SUR spokesman said: "We had to be very careful not to offend Muslim sensibilities." Guests were given gloves, scarves and bags of sweets. They were handed cups of Earl Grey tea as they left.

Party guest Jamal Shajhee, 16, from Afghanistan, told The Sun: "Tonight I will try to make my way to England because there are many benefits there for me."

Local residents slammed the bash. Laurent Fonck, 39, said: "More will come here if they know they will be well looked after."

Headline *Oh come all ye:* from a Christmas song 'Oh come all ye faithful' (Herbei o ihr Gläubigen)
2 *sneak:* schleichen
2 *treat sb. to sth.:* give sb. sth. they enjoy
5 *gift:* Geschenk
6 *carol:* Christmas song
7 *offend sb.:* jdn. beleidigen
10 *sleep rough:* sleep outside
15 *in defiance of:* against
22 *turkey:* Truthahn
24 *sensibilities:* feelings
27 *benefits:* Sozialleistungen
28 *slam sth.:* critise sth. strongly
28 *bash:* party
Photo caption
(a) cracker:
1. (infml.) spitze;
2. Knallbonbon
scoff sth.: verschlingen

H Understanding the news article

Summarise the relevant facts about the party referred to in the article.

Wrintten texts
▶ 2.2c

I Analysing the news article

When you studied Articles 1 and 2, you saw that one article reported facts, the other gave a newspaper's opinion. Article 3 is another news article. The question is: does it just report facts or does it also try to influence the reader (i.e. indirectly express an opinion)? In other words, is the article 'fair and balanced' or 'biased'?

Work with a partner or in a group to analyse how events and people are presented in the article and the effect that this has on the reader. Then use your findings to characterise the writer's intentions when he wrote this article.

	WHAT IS STRESSED BY MENTIONING THESE DETAILS?	INTENDED EFFECT ON THE READER
THE PARTY - *guests mainly Muslim asylum seekers* - *food, presents, etc.* - *Ethiopia's national anthem* - *no Christmas traditions (turkey, carols …)*	- *asylum seekers well-treated* - *respect for asylum seekers' religion and customs*	*The writer highlights / emphasises / stresses / underlines … / repeats / gives the reader the impression that / leaves the reader with the idea that / suggests / implies that …*
THE ASYLUM SEEKERS AND THEIR REACTIONS TO THE PARTY - *trying to 'sneak' into UK* - *sleeping rough because no lorries* - *J. Shajhee: "I will … benefits there for me."*	- *this is illegal and dishonest* - … - …	…
OTHER INFORMATION - *how the 'jungle' camp began* - *Sangatte II* - *reactions of local people*	… … …	
STRUCTURE / PICTURES - *use of headlines* - *final sentence* - *photo and photo caption (the word 'scoff')*	… … …	

Written texts
▶ 5.2e

J Reacting to the news article

Imagine that you are from the local C'SUR charity that organised this party. Write to the editor of *The Sun* expressing your opinion about this article.

3 Talking about news and newspapers (A discussion)

You are going to discuss some of the issues about news and newspapers you have studied in this topic using an activity called 'Walk-Talk-Write'.

Activity chest
▶ 15

1. Put up four large pieces of paper around your classroom. At the top of these are the questions you can see below.

HOW WELL-INFORMED DO YOU FEEL YOU ARE ABOUT IMPORTANT WORLD EVENTS? (WHY?)

ARE ARTICLES LIKE THE ONE FROM THE SUN 'DANGEROUS'? (WHY? / WHY NOT?)

COULD NEWSPAPERS MAKE NEWS MORE INTERESTING TO TEENAGERS? (HOW?)

SHOULD NEWSPAPERS WRITE ABOUT THE PRIVATE LIVES OF FAMOUS PEOPLE? (WHY? / WHY NOT?)

2. Work in groups first to collect your ideas about all the questions, then go round the classroom in your groups writing up your ideas and reacting to those of other students.

Written texts
▶ 5.1

3. Talk in class about the ideas that were expressed during the activity. What general picture emerged of the class's opinions (what opinions did large numbers of people agree on)? Did any of the opinions you read surprise you? Have any of the things you studied in this topic changed the way you now feel about news and newspapers? If so, how?

Reporting the news

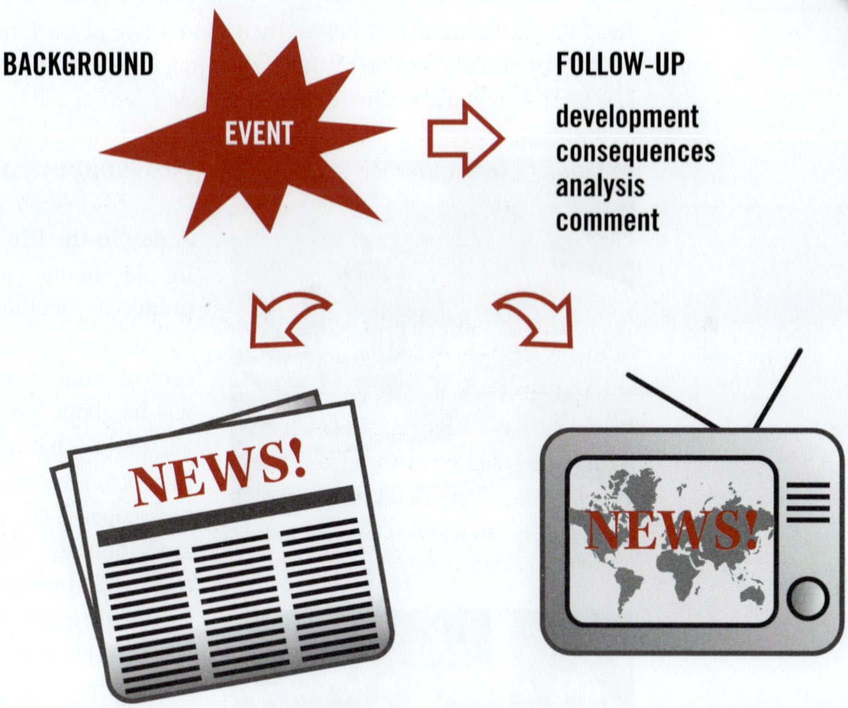

The main part of any news story is an event – something that happens. But behind this event there is a background situation. The event may also go on for a certain time and it can always have consequences. After the event, too, there is time to think about it. Newspapers and TV news programmes cover all of this.

Working in groups and on projects
▶ 1

Collect ideas

1. Work with a partner or in a small group. Think of a news story that you know about. Using it as an example, describe the main event, the background, how the story could develop (and any consquences of it), and what aspects of the story reporters might want to analyse and comment on. Present your example to the class.
2. News stories are reported in newspapers and on TV news programmes. These are two very different media, however. Compare them using a chart like the one below. Characterise them as a medium, say how long after an event they report it, and when / where / how people read or watch the news report. Identify what you think are the key strengths and weaknesses of each.

NEWSPAPERS	TV NEWS PROGRAMMES
- *written / printed words* - …	- …

1 How journalists write (Newspaper news articles)

You are going to watch a video of a journalist explaining how a news story is written, and then look in detail at two articles.

A Before you watch

Read the background text below, then choose two of the kinds of people mentioned in it and write a short profile of them: their job, where they work, typical tasks at work. Use your own words – the 'No copying!' rule.

The newsroom. This is where the news is written and edited

A press conference. Reporters gather information for their news stories

Newspapers at work

A day in the life of a newspaper

In 24 hours, a typical newspaper produces something that is longer than the average paperback book. Ninety per cent of what appears in the newspaper will be about 'new' events – it is, after all, 'news'. That means that even before they begin writing, the journalists on the newspaper have to gather information (and photos) for a story by doing research, interviewing people, and frequently going to press conferences. Writing the newspaper is still not the end of the story, however. It has to be printed and then distributed so its readers can buy it. It is normally over a year before a paperback book appears in the bookshops. A newspaper does the same thing in a day – six days a week.

Who's who in a newspaper office

Journalists are the 'eyes and ears' of the newspaper, but behind them there are other people who make the newspaper possible. Most important are the editors. Various editors have different jobs. The main editor has the top job. He or she decides which stories to report. Below this person are other editors (each news category usually has its own) whose job it is to fit the article on to the page. This often involves cutting it to the right length. These editors also usually write the headline for the story. Editors work in the newsroom where the reporters come to write their stories.

8 *gather sth.:* collect sth.
9 *research:* process of discovering new information
14 *distribute sth.:* send sth. out to different places
23 *editor:* Redakteur/in

Parts of a newspaper article

Journalists use specific terms to describe the various parts of the articles they write.

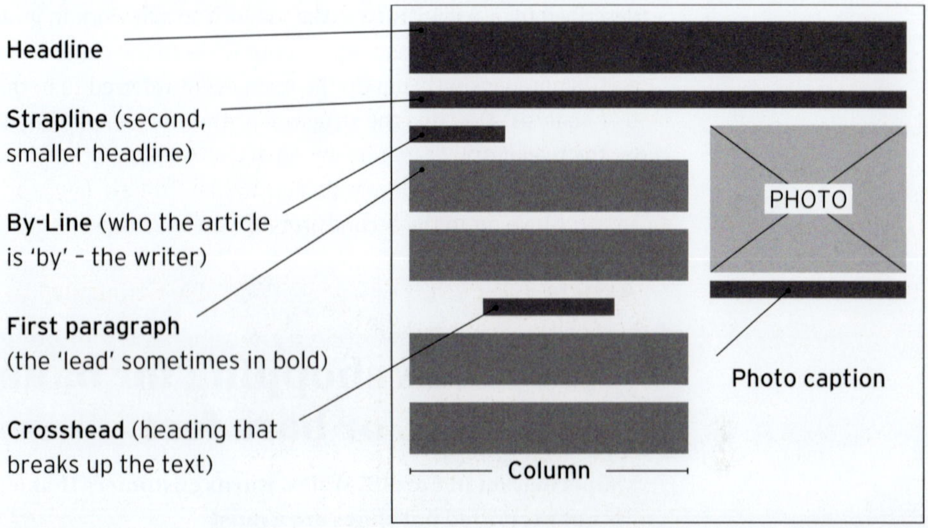

DVD 10

Sound and (moving) images ▶ 1.2

B Watch the video

D'Arcy Drury is an American journalist and teacher, working in the Middle East.

1. Copy and complete the grid below.
2. Compare with a partner. Watch again and check, then give an oral summary of the video.

DEFINITION OF 'HARD NEWS'	
THREE WAYS OF WRITING (WITH EXAMPLES)	1. …
DIAGRAM OF THE INVERTED PYRAMID	*LEAD (= most …)*
ADVANTAGES OF THE INVERTED PYRAMID STYLE	- *journalists* - *readers*
ADVICE FOR STUDENTS	

Notes on the video
inverted pyramid: umgekehrte Pyramide
flip sth. around = invert sth.
in descending order: nach Wichtigkeit geordnet
entire: whole, complete
facilitate sth.: make sth. easy

Drury begins by … -ing …
He then goes on to explain / describe / tell us about …
He uses the following example(s) / illustrations to clarify what he means: …
He ends by …-ing … / Finally, he …

[Video clip from: Abu Dhabi Men's College, UAE]

C Understanding and analysing two news articles

Use the following hard news stories to illustrate the style of journalistic writing described by d'Arcy Drury in the video. You can work in groups, each group taking a different article, and then report your ideas to the class. For each article:

a (Comprehension) Sum up the main event referred to in the article.

b (Analysis) Describe the structure of the story, explaining the advantages this has for the reader.

✕ **Extra:** Move on to the second story if you have time.

Article 1

Tesco bans shopping for bananas in pyjamas … or bare feet

Supermarket in Cardiff, Wales, warns customers that nightwear is not permitted but shoes are a must

Pyjamas and bare feet may be OK around home but a Tesco supermarket in Cardiff is concerned they may offend other customers.

Customers at a Welsh branch of Tesco have been banned from shopping in their pyjamas or bare feet.

Notices have been put up in the St Mellons store in Cardiff saying: "Footwear must be worn at all times and no nightwear is permitted."

A spokesman said Tesco did not have a strict dress code, but it did not want people shopping in their nightwear in case it offended other customers.

He said he was not aware of any other Tesco stores having to put up similar signs.

"We're not a nightclub with a strict dress code, and jeans and trainers are of course more than welcome."

"We do, however, request that customers do not shop in their PJs or nightgowns. This is to avoid causing offence or embarrassment to others."

Tesco is not the first store to ban customers from shopping in their nightwear. In 2008 a Dublin cafe erected a "no pyjamas" sign, and in 2006 the Gulf emirate of Ras al-Khaimah introduced a new dress code to stop people wearing their sleep suits to work.

More than 10,600 people have joined a Facebook group called "STOP GIRLS AND WOMEN WEARING PYJAMAS ON THE STREETS OF LIVERPOOL!!!!!", and last year an Irish production company made a documentary called The Pyjama Girls, about a group of teenagers living in central Dublin who spend most of their time in pyjamas.

[From: The Independent, 21 September 2009]

Headline *Tesco:* UK's largest supermarket chain
bare: naked
4 *offend sb.:* make sb. upset or angry
13 *dress code:* rules about what can/can't be worn
23 *nightgown:* Morgenmantel
24 *embarrassment:* Verlegenheit
27 *erect sth:* put sth. up, build sth.

Article 2

Bathwater saves Haiti survivor after 15 days

METRO REPORTER

A teenage girl pulled alive from a collapsed house 15 days after the Haitian earthquake survived by drinking water from a bath.

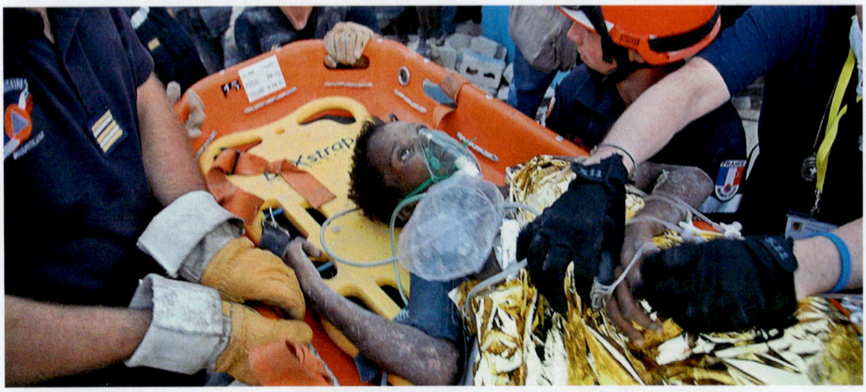

Darlene Etienne, 17, is treated at a French military field hospital after being rescued from a collapsed building by a French search and rescue team in Port-au-Prince

Darlene Etienne, 17, cried with joy as she was dragged from rubble in a severely dehydrated state. She could only say "thank you" to rescuers as crowds cheered and clapped her on her way to a waiting ambulance.

Darlene was trapped between a collapsed wall and a door in the remains of her home in the quake-flattened capital of Port-au-Prince. She owes her life to a passer-by who heard her voice and urged Red Cross and civil protection workers to send rescuers to the site.

"I don't know how she happened to resist that long. It's a miracle," said rescue worker JP Malaganne. "She will live, she has her whole life ahead of her," said Col Michel Orcel, a French doctor. "We are providing the care she needs and she will be OK."

Her French rescue crew shouted: "We are the best team in the world" after she was taken to a field hospital. "It's not at all usual. It's exceptional," added crew member Stephan Sadak. More than 130 people have been rescued from the rubble since the quake hit on January 12. The number has surprised experts who were more pessimistic about survival rates. Haitians are still appealing to search teams to go to new sites.

Meanwhile, the country's government appealed to foreign leaders and charities to do more to help the earthquake victims. "I am not in a position to criticise anybody, not in the least people who have come here to help me," said President Rene Preval. "What I am saying is, what everybody is saying is, that we need a better coordination."

[From: Metro.co.uk, February 2010

Headlines
earthquake: Erdbeben
collapse: fall down
1 *rubble:* stones, bricks etc. from fallen buildings
1 *drag sb./sth.:* pull sb./sth.
1 *severely dehydrated state:* when your body has lost a lot of water
4 *trapped:* eingeklemmt
4 *remains:* Überreste
5 *quake-flattened:* made flat by the earthquake
5 *owe one's life to sb.:* be alive because of sb.
6 *civil protection worker:* person who works to protect citizens
7 *site:* place
8 *resist:* (here) stay alive
8 *miracle:* Wunder
16 *appeal to sb.:* jdn. dringend bitten
19 *victim:* Opfer

2 How television reports the news (A TV news story)

You are going to watch an extract from a British TV news programme: *Channel 4 News.*

A Before you begin

Read the introduction to the extract. Imagine you are the reporter who has to make a 5-minute report for the programme. Taking into account the situation, suggest what you might put into your report and why. Think particularly about how much viewers already know about the main event and how you can do a follow-up report.

Waveland: a video report

The main event

In August 2005, a massive hurricane (Hurricane Katrina) hit New Orleans in the southern USA, destroying houses and flooding streets in the city and in many other smaller towns in the surrounding area. Almost 2,000 people died in the catastrophe and many thousands more were left homeless.

Your situation

You are a British TV reporter, Jonathan Rugman. You are based permanently in the USA (reporters like this are called 'correspondents') and you work for one of Britain's TV channels, *Channel 4*. Its early-evening news programme lasts an hour and is well respected for the quality of its news.

It is now a few days after the hurricane. You have been sent to a small town near New Orleans called Waveland to make a report. The eye of the hurricane passed right through the town.

The Hurricane Katrina story is so important that on this evening the whole news programme is being broadcast live from New Orleans and the programme's anchorman, Jon Snow, will introduce your report.

20 *broadcast (a programme):* senden

Correspondent Jonathan Rugman

Channel 4 News anchorman, Jon Snow, presenting the programme live from New Orleans

Photo caption *anchorman:* Moderator einer Nachrichtensendung

DVD 11

Sound and (moving) images ▶ 1.2

Activity chest ▶ 13

B Understanding and analysing the video

1. Watch the whole video once for a general understanding. Sum up what it shows in a few sentences in your own words.
2. Watch the video again for a more detailed understanding of the content and to analyse important aspects of it as a TV news report. Use the grid below which shows the report's 'storyboard' – the sections or 'segments' into which it is divided.
   a Work with a partner. Make a copy of the grid. Partner A: as you watch, write in roughly how long each segment lasts (for example, 1 min 20 secs). Partner B: take notes into your grid about what happens in each segment. When you have finished, compare your grid with that of another pair of students. Then share your ideas with the class.

SEGMENT	NOTES
1 Anchorman Jon Snow in New Orleans / Jonathan Rugman in Waveland Length:	*- JS introduces JR* *- JR tells us about Waveland / mentions President Bush.*
2 President George Bush Length:	
3 Views of Waveland Length:	…
4 Brian Mollere Length:	*- Mollere tells us about …* *- We also see his neighbour who …*
5 Supermarket car park Length:	
6 Waveland's local chemist Length:	
7 Susan St Amant Length:	
8 Railway track in Waveland Length:	
9 Jon Snow (anchorman) Length:	

   b Watch the video again and go back to your ideas from task A on the last page. Compare these with what the reporter actually reported.

The report:
gives / doesn't give a lot of background information because …
shows the situation in the area all around New Orleans / uses a specific example of (a town) to illustrate the general situation in …
gives a lot of dry facts and figures / personalises the situation by …-ing … (for example, …).
talks about the situations / shows viewers pictures of the situation.
The effect of all this on viewers is …

3. This time watch the video in two groups. Each group will concentrate on a different aspect of it and report to the class.

Sound and (moving) images
▶ 3.1-5

GROUP A: You are going to look at the technical aspects of the video. Using your grid of the different segments again, watch and find examples of the following techniques. Analyse why Jonathan Rugman uses them, and the effect each has on the viewer.

straight to camera: when a reporter looks at the camera and talks directly to viewers

SHOTS	straight to camera / panning shot / tracking shot / close-up / low-angle shot / over-the-shoulder shot / visual detail (e.g. a close-up of a flag)
SOUND	voiceover / interviewer's questions off screen
OTHER	names of people on screen / use of anchorman

GROUP B: You are going to answer the question: 'What impression of Waveland and its inhabitants does the report give viewers and how does it convey this impression?' Consider the following points:

- Is it sympathetic to the people of Waveland? How does it show this?
- Is it critical of the American government?
- How would you characterise the tone of the report? Examples? Why?
- Does it make America seem different in any way from Europe?
- What is the role of the anchorman and the reporter himself in the report?

C Writing about the video

Activity chest
▶ 11

Write an answer to one of questions a-e below. Then make groups of students who answered the same question and use 'Peer review' to check and improve your answer. Present one of your answers to the class.

(Comprehension)

a Outline the effect of the hurricane on the town of Waveland.

b Point out the impact of the hurricane on the lives of the residents of Waveland.

c Summarise the information about the help that the residents of Waveland are – or in their eyes are not - being given to rebuild their lives.

(Analysis)

d Illustrate with examples how the video uses technical devices such as voiceover, close-ups and visual details to report a story. Explain the effect these devices have on the viewer.

e Explain with examples how the video gives a picture of the events through the material the reporter chooses to include in the report.

D Reacting to the video

intrusive: looking too deeply into a person's private life

1. Talk in class. Discuss how you feel about TV news programmes showing us personal human tragedies - people like Susan St Amant, for example, while she is crying. Say whether you feel this is any way intrusive.

Written texts
▶ 5.2e

2. Use the information in the video to write a newspaper news story about the event.

[Video clip from: Channel 4 News]

E Check your grammar 2 (Reported speech)

Grammar you can use
▶ 1.7

Answers
▶ p. 172

You are a newspaper reporter who has just attended a press conference given by a U.S. government spokesperson about the disaster in New Orleans. Rewrite the speaker's words in reported speech for use in your article. Use different reporting verbs from the box to add variety.

add – admit – emphasise - explain – go on to say – maintain – promise – say (that) – state – stress – tell (reporters) – warn

SPOKESPERSON TOM LEDERMAN: "This is the biggest catastrophe in the history of the Mississippi area. So far 1,476 people have died. Thousands more are homeless. The disaster is so immense that reacting to it is an almost impossible task. However, we are doing everything we can to help people. The army and medical services are in the area, and yesterday the government set aside $2 billion dollars to rebuild the area. More help will arrive in the next few days. We will let you have more information as soon as it is available. Thank you."

F Increase your wordpower (Adjectives to describe news)

1. Look at the words in the boxes below. Classify as many as you can under three headings: *positive*, *negative* and *neutral*. Compare with a partner.

EVENTS	amazing – amusing – appalling – catastrophic – depressing – disastrous – dramatic – exciting – funny – heart-rending – hilarious – impressive – incredible – mind-blowing – sad – sensational – spectacular – staggering – stirring – tense – terrible – thrilling – tragic
NEWS REPORTS	accurate – authoritative – balanced – biased – clear – compassionate – convincing – critical – dramatic – dry – dull – educational – emotional – entertaining – factual – fair – inaccurate – informal – interpretive – lively – matter-of-fact – moderate – objective – observant – persuasive – precise – reassuring – reliable – restrained – sentimental – slick – spontaneous – subjective – subtle – unbiased – unreliable – unsentimental – visually interesting

2. Look back through the news stories and events that you have read about so far in this sequence. Use the sentence patterns below to describe them.
I think the most … (the …-est) story we have read about is …
Another … story has been the one about …
My favourite story has been X because it was so …
Some stories have been extremely / truly / absolutely … For example, the X story.
Some of the articles we have read have been … while others have been … For example, …
I liked the article / video about X because it was so …

G Final activity

Written texts
▶ 5.2e

Write your own news. Write a newspaper article or make a radio report about a hard news event. It can be something that happened in your town or your school, or an event that you know about generally. If possible, do some research (for example, by interviewing people, looking in your local newspaper or going online). Or you may invent details yourself.

TOPIC 03

Who reports the news?

London, 27 July 2005. Terrorists explode bombs in the Underground and another bomb goes off on this bus. Photos like this appear soon afterwards on the BBC and other TV channels, and are on the front pages of all the newspapers the next day. The thing is, that this photo was not taken by a journalist, but by a member of the public – an 'ordinary person'. Moreover, the photo (together with news stories) was on the internet on blogs and social networking sites long before it reached the mass media. The people reporting the news were not traditional journalists, but a new kind of reporter called a 'citizen journalist'.

Collect ideas

Collect your ideas in groups in a copy of the chart below, then report to the class.

	TRADITIONAL REPORTING (MASS MEDIA)	CITIZEN JOURNALISM
TECHNOLOGIES USED	- *printing* - *TV*	…
WHEN / WHERE REPORTED		*immediately / online*
WHO REPORTS THE NEWS		
POSSIBLE ADVANTAGES		
POSSIBLE DISADVANTAGES		

✕ **Extra:** Imagine you are there when an important event takes place. You have a mobile phone with a camera. Describe the event, what you do and your feelings.

An examination of citizen journalism
(Blogs and newspaper articles)

You are going to look in detail at citizen journalism through four articles. Two are blogs, two are newspaper articles (one is in German). Your aim is to form an opinion of how important this new development is in the media world.

Activity chest ▶ 6

A Working with the texts

1. Study and share information about the texts with 'Expert groups'.
   a Study the texts in groups, using the following chart to collect information and prepare a summary.

SUBJECT	*The text is about …*
BACKGROUND	*The background to the text is …*
TEXT TYPE	*The text is a blog / a newspaper article.*
AIM OF TEXT	*The writer aims to give an opinion about … / report about …*
CONTENT	*The main points of the text are …*
SUMMARY	*So, to sum all that up briefly, …*

   b Share the information in the usual way. When you return to your original groups, sum up the information you now have (news event or article / main points you learned / importance of these main points), then compare the advantages and disadvantages of citizen journalism using a copy of the chart below.

CITIZEN JOURNALISM COMPARED TO TRADITIONAL JOURNALISM	
ADVANTAGES	DISADVANTAGES
- *can cover stories that professional journalists can't because …* - …	- *can sometimes be inaccurate because …* - …

Activity chest ▶ 10

2. Discuss the pros and cons of citizen journalism with a 'Panel discussion'. Consider this idea in your discussion: 'One day most news will come from citizen journalists'. (This is called 'the motion'.)
   - First collect arguments for and against the motion in A and B groups.
   - Then divide into smaller groups to prepare ideas on specific aspects of your argument.
   - Choose your group representatives and hold the discussion.
   - Vote at the end for or against the motion.

✕ **Extra:** You often post comments on an internet forum. At the moment there is a discussion about the importance of citizen journalism. Write a text for the forum.

Article 1: The Hudson River plane crash (A blog)

Written texts
▶ 2.2b

In the afternoon of 15 January 2009, a US Airways Airbus took off from LaGuardia Airport, New York. At around 1,000 meters, the plane hit a flock of birds and both engines stopped working. Unable to return to LaGuardia or to reach another airport, the pilot safely crash-landed the plane in the Hudson River next to downtown Manhattan. None of the 155 passengers on board was killed and the pilot and his crew were later described as heroes.

flock of birds: Vogelschwarm

HOW THE HUDSON RIVER PLANE CRASH BROUGHT US TOGETHER

In case you were in any doubt, last night's dramatic plane crash-landing in the Hudson River in New York provided yet more proof about how interconnected we all are in the internet age.

The major media outlets in New York responded quickly and on the whole they did a good job of reporting the news of the so-called 'miracle on the Hudson'.

Yet the most immediate and compelling reports and images came from citizens. Even if you had the most rapid response system in the world, reporters were not able to teleport themselves to the scene - not to mention the fact that the on-the-ground location changed as the plane floated downstream.

By contrast, news was all over microblogging website Twitter within minutes. One of the early reports came from New Yorker Janis Krum who wrote: "There's a plane in the Hudson. I'm on the ferry going to pick up the people. Crazy." Krum also uploaded this pic of the plane floating in the river. Krum was interviewed by MSNBC later yesterday and his pic had more than 100,000 views on TwitPic by this morning.

I didn't follow Krum at the time, but within about 10 minutes of first hearing about the plane crash, my Twitter friends were sending me messages pointing me to Krum's post. It's possible that either people who followed Krum already were repeating (or retweeting) his posts, or that they'd found his post by searching on a service such as Summize. Either way, it was impressively fast - and it was great hearing about it first-hand at a point in time when we weren't sure if everyone had survived.

Although I did some of my own browsing on my favourite news websites to try to figure out what was going on, again Twitter proved itself as an excellent news aggregator, pointing me to links to the best media coverage. I particularly appreciated the live video streaming on CNN.com and MSNBC.com among others.

[From: The Guardian, 16 January 2009]

8 *media outlet:* Medienunternehmen
12 *compelling:* fascinating and convincing
14 *teleport sb.:* transport sb. extremely fast
20 *MSNBC:* American news network, Microsoft National Broadcasting Company
20 *TwitPic:* part of the Twitter site for photos
23 *point sb. to sth.:* show sb. where to go
26 *impressive:* beeindruckend
30 *figure sth. out:* understand sth.
30 *news aggregator:* website that brings various data together in one place
31 *media coverage:* Berichterstattung in den Medien
32 *appreciate sth.:* etwas schätzen
32 *CNN:* American news network, Cable News Network

Article 2: Protests in Iran (A newspaper article)

In June 2009, elections took place in Iran to choose a new national leader. The country's leader was re-elected, but many Iranians believed that the elections had not been fair. Protests were organised around the country, especially in the capital Tehran, and during these, protesters were often brutally attacked by the police.

When Iran's regime falls this will be remembered as the YouTube revolution

Adam LeBor: Analysis

When the Iranian regime eventually crumbles, as all tyrannies must, the events that brought it down will be remembered as the first YouTube revolution. Once uploaded on to the internet, the snatched, grainy video footage, the camera angle lurching up and down and from side to side, has an instant impact, both domestically and internationally.

[...]

News is pouring out despite the best efforts of the Iranian censors. The monitoring centre is believed to engage in a process called Deep Packet Inspection, which deconstructs every packet of digitised data, examines it for keywords such as 'democracy' and 'freedom' and then reconstructs it within seconds. This enables the Government to monitor protesters' activities, block communications and gather information. But in this continuing cat-and-mouse game the opposition is winning.

Many are using proxy servers to connect to the internet and either email or upload their films. Proxy servers are servers that act as intermediaries for internet users seeking to access banned sites.

[...]

"Citizen journalists in Iran are technically very savvy. They send their films and pictures out to their contacts, who upload the material for them. The internet is hugely important in getting information out of Iran, and for people in smaller cities there to know what is happening," said Golnaz Esfandiari, an Iranian-born journalist for Radio Free Europe/Radio Liberty, based in Prague.

[...]

The growth in computing power, internet bandwidth and easy access to communications technology is changing the balance of power not just in Iran, but in all countries with repressive regimes. Dictators, take note.

[From: The Times, 29 December 2009]

2 *crumble:* fall to pieces, end
6 *snatched:* (video) taken very quickly
6 *grainy:* grobkörnig
6 *video footage:* video pictures
9 *domestic:* at home
14 *monitoring centre:* Überwachungszentrum
14 *engage in sth.:* (here) use sth.
15 *inspection:* Kontrolle
15 *deconstruct sth.:* etwas zerlegen
18 *reconstruct sth.:* etwas wiederherstellen
25 *proxy server:* part of the worldwide computer network that receives and sends on data
28 *intermediary:* Vermittler
32 *savvy:* clever, well-informed
45 *balance of power:* Machtverhältnis, Gleichgewicht der Mächte
47 *repressive:* unterdrückerisch

Article 3: The 'death' of Steve Jobs (A blog)

Written texts
▶ 2.2b

CNN, based in the U.S. in Atlanta, New York, Washington, D.C and Los Angeles, is one of the world's best-known news broadcasters. Started in 1980, it was the first TV channel anywhere to broadcast 24-hour news. In August 2006, the channel launched a new service, iReport. This gives citizen journalists the chance to post their own news and pictures online on the CNN website. It was on iReport that, in 2008, a report appeared about the sudden death of Steve Jobs, the founder of Apple Inc., and the man behind Apple Mac computers and the iPhone. The report shocked people around the world.

FALSE HEART ATTACK REPORT A STEP BACKWARD FOR CITIZEN JOURNALISM

Friday October 3, 2008

Citizen journalism took a hit Friday when a CNN iReport poster falsely claimed Apple CEO Steve Jobs had suffered a heart attack.

According to Silicon Valley Insider, an iReport user named 'johntw' claimed Jobs had been rushed to the ER after a severe heart attack. But an Apple spokeswoman categorically denied the report, and the post was removed from the website.

CNN responded that "iReport.com is an entirely user-generated site where the content is determined by the community. Content that does not comply with Community Guidelines will be removed. After the content in question was uploaded to iReport.com, the community brought it to our attention. Based on our Terms of Use that govern user behavior on iReport.com, the fraudulent content was removed from the site and the user's account was disabled."

The Wall Street Journal's 'Marketbeat' blog reported that Apple shares briefly plunged to $94.65 following the report, then recovered. This is a particularly sensitive issue for Apple and Jobs, who battled cancer several years ago.

Needless to say, nothing could be more damaging to the credibility of citizen journalists than a prank like this. This incident illustrates the need for more careful monitoring of websites like iReport, both by the companies that host them and by citizen journalists themselves. Indeed, those who use sites like iReport have everything to gain by ensuring that falsehoods aren't spread across the web under the banner of citizen journalism.

[From: About.com, 3 October 2008]

5 *Silicon Valley Insider:* blog based in the hi-tech region Silicon Valley, south of San Francisco
7 *rush sb.:* take sb. somewhere quickly
7 *ER:* Notaufnahme
8 *heart attack:* Herzinfarkt
9 *deny sth.:* etwas dementieren
13 *determine sth.* decide sth., control sth.
13 *comply with sth.:* etwas entsprechen
16 *Terms of Use:* rules
16 *govern sth.:* etwas regeln
16 *fraudulent:* falsch, betrügerisch
17 *disable sth.:* stop sth. from working
18 *shares:* Aktien
19 *plunge:* fall quickly
21 *needless to say:* naturally, of course
21 *credibility:* Glaubwürdigkeit
22 *prank:* silly trick
25 *gain sth.:* win sth.
25 *falsehood:* lie
26 *banner:* flag

Article 4: An experiment (Mediation)

This article describes an experiment organised by several radio stations.

Allein mit Twitter und Facebook – ein Experiment

Von Victor Henle Düsseldorf

Auf einem Bauernhof im Périgord ging in Frankreich gerade eine ungewöhnliche Art eines Big-Brother-Experiments zu Ende. Fünf französischsprachige Journalisten aus Frankreich, Kanada, Belgien und der Schweiz schlossen sich fünf Tage mit der Absicht ein, sich nur mit Facebook und Twitter über die Außenwelt zu informieren. Sie wollten erproben, was sie unter diesen Umständen über die Welt erfahren. Das Experiment lief unter Titel: „Eingeschlossen im Netz".

Eine allgemeine Schlussfolgerung lautet: Traditionelle Medien und soziale Netzwerke ersetzen sich gegenseitig nicht, sondern sind komplementär. Einige wichtige Einzelerkenntnisse drängten sich den Journalisten jedoch auf. Erstaunt waren sie über die Geschwindigkeit, mit der sich Twitter-Nachrichten ausbreiten. Ein Journalist brachte das Beispiel eines Mannes, der in Russland plötzlich festgenommen wurde und davon vor der Polizeistation gerade noch einen Journalisten mit seinem Smartphone informieren konnte.

Nachrichten gelangen oft ungeprüft in die Netzwerke

Gleichzeitig erschreckte die „Eingeschlossenen" des Périgord die Vorstellung, wie leicht ungeprüfte Nachrichten in die Netzwerke gelangen können. Die Meldung etwa, in der Stadt Lille habe es eine Explosion gegeben, veranlasste über 5000 Nutzer, sich einer Facebook-Gruppe anzuschließen. Später stellte sich heraus, dass es nur der Knall eines Flugzeuges war [...]

Eine andere wichtige Erkenntnis war, wie sehr die Informationsbreite und die Erklärfunktion der traditionellen Medien fehlten. So wurden bei Zitaten von Politikern oft Hintergrund und Kontext vermisst, in denen diese Äußerungen fielen.

Aufgefallen ist den Teilnehmern auch die andersartige Hierarchie der Nachrichten. während sonst der Bahnstreik das mediale Hauptthema war, rangierte bei Twitter die bunte Nachricht an erster Stelle, die französische Justizministerin Alliot-Marie und ihr Kollege, der Innenminister Brice Hortefeux, könnten sich nicht ausstehen.

Ein Mangel war evident: Auslandsnachrichten drangen fast keine zu den Probanden. Anscheinend interessieren sich die Nutzer der sozialen Netzwerke mehr für die kleinen Dinge des Lebens im eigenen Land als für das, was außerhalb der Grenzen geschieht. Der kanadische Journalist fasste seine Erfahrung so zusammen: „Es ist verrückt, wie viel Aufwand wir treiben mussten, um ein kleines bisschen Informationen zu bekommen, die wir in den alten Medien selbstverständlich gehabt hätten."

[From: Rheinische Post, 12 February 2010]

TOPIC

04

Welcome to the dark side

The internet is, of course, a wonderful thing. But does it have a 'dark side'?

Collect ideas

Talk in class.

1. Point out some of the advantages of the internet and how it can be a positive thing in teenagers' lives.
2. Discuss how important the internet is in your life personally . Imagine that for one whole month you had to live without it. How difficult would that be? Would it, in fact, make a difference to your life? Would you actually be happier without it?
3. In groups, list some of the 'dangers' of the internet you often hear about. Tell the class what they are and in what ways they can affect teenagers' lives.

Working in groups and on projects ▶ 1

The internet has a great many advantages for young people such as …	
But / However / Despite this, though,	there can be certain dangers / threats / risks …
For example, one danger that	teenagers can face / come across online is …
Another possible / potential hazard is …	
This can have a	terrible / catastrophic / disastrous effect on … because …
For example, …	

1 Cyberfriends (A blog article)

You are going to read an article from a blog which keeps its readers informed of internet trends and analyses how the internet influences people's lives. This article is about teenagers and cyberfriends.

A Before you read

Talk in class.
- Define the term 'cyberfriend', constrasting it with a 'real-life friend'.
- Describe any personal experiences you have of cyberfriends.

YOUR 'REAL' FRIENDS ARE YOUR ONLINE FRIENDS (OR SO SAYS GEN Y)

Written by Sarah Perez / August 10, 2009 7:17 AM / 27 Comments

Is it easier to talk to your online buddies than your friends out there in the 'real world'? Do you feel like you know more about what's happening in the lives of your Facebook and MySpace friends than with those who don't have accounts or don't bother to update them? According to a recent UK MySpace study of over 16,000 social network users, these sorts of feelings are common among today's younger generation. The study revealed that a good portion of this group admits to feeling more comfortable sharing and communicating with friends online than they do when logged out of cyberspace.

Online: Sharing is Easier, Friends Know You Better

The MySpace study asked social networking users between the ages of 14 and 21 (aka 'Generation Y') questions about their interactions both on social networks and in their real life, too. Some 36 % of the respondents said they found it easier to talk about themselves online than in the real world, leading them to share more about themselves using technology. This group also felt that their online friends knew more about them, and so, in a sense, were closer than offline friends because they all knew what was going on in each other's lives.

Outside of the social networking sites, the survey respondents overwhelmingly felt ill-at-ease in social groups. A whopping 72 % said they felt 'left out' and didn't think they fit into any particular group. More than four-fifths (82 %) said they moved between four or more different groups of friends in an effort to find acceptance.

12 *aka* = also known as
13 *repondent:* person who replies to questions in a survey
16 *in a sense:* gewissermaßen
18 *overwhelmingly:* mit großer Mehrheit
19 *ill-at-ease:* nervous, uncomfortable
19 *whopping:* extremely large
21 *in an effort to:* trying to

It's not entirely surprising that the younger generation feels this way. The teen years (and young adulthood to some extent) are a time when kids start exploring and experimenting with many different aspects of their personalities, as they attempt to solidify who they are and who they will become as adults. What's interesting, though, is how social networking is having an impact on this traditional coming-of-age process. Instead of simply feeling disjointed, confused, and lonely, today's younger generation has an outlet for connecting with their peers which previous generations did not: the internet.

Says Rebekah Horne, MySpace Europe managing director, the study provides insight into how this generation is "using online as a way to explore and settle into their burgeoning identities."

But at what cost?

Will the younger generations remain awkward and shy in the real world as they age, only finding comfort in their interactions that occur online? Or does having an outlet for their feelings simply lessen the blow delivered by the otherwise often harsh process that is growing up?

In many ways, easy access to technology can be seen as both a blessing and a curse for this young group of digital natives. These days, you'll often encounter teens having text message conversations or posting status updates, while ignoring the very friends they're present with in the real world. Behaviour like this could certainly send a message to the others that they are second priority to whomever else has engaged their friend's attention. That could easily lead to feelings of being 'left out' as reported in this study.

And yet, at the same time, it's this very technology that's allowing the teens and young adults to feel like they have friends who know them and care about them. The issue is balancing that online life with the one out in the real world.

The question as to whether this sort of behaviour is healthy is one best left to psychologists to analyze and report, but there's no doubt that at the very least, it is having an impact.

26 *solidify sth.:* make sth. solid
28 *coming-of-age process:* Prozess des Erwachsenwerdens
28 *disjointed:* not belonging to any group
32 *settle into sth.:* feel at home in a situation
33 *burgeoning:* growing, developing
35 *awkward:* unbeholfen
37 *lessen the blow:* make a situation less hard
37 *otherwise:* ansonsten
38 *harsh:* rau
39 *a blessing and a curse:* Segen und Fluch
40 *encounter sb.:* meet sb.
43 *second priority:* zweitrangig
44 *whomever else:* wer auch immer
48 *balance sth. with sth.:* ein Gleichgewicht herstellen/halten zwischen

[From: ReadWriteWeb, 10 August 2009]

B Understanding the text

Answer these questions.

a Point out the advantages for teenagers of online friends according to the article.

b Outline what the writer says in this article about the possible dangers for teens of online friendships.

Extra: Work in groups. Choose an important issue or situation referred to in the text and use a 'Freeze-frame' tableau to bring it to life.

Activity chest ▶ 8

C Analysing the text

Written texts
▶ 2.2b

1. Explain the writer's intention when writing this post.
2. Analyse how the writer attempts to achieve her goals with regard to her intentions. Bear the following in mind:
   - how she tries to get and keep the readers' attention,
   - how the article is structured to convey its message to the readers,
   - what facts the article is based on and why,
   - to what extent the author includes her personal opinion,
   - whether the writer suggests a solution to the problems referred to in the post.

D Reacting to the text

Activity chest
▶ 14

Based on your personal experience, which points do you agree or disagree with in the post? Work in groups to hold a 'Silent discussion'. Each person should first write down something they agree with in the post. Then 'reply' to those ideas and add others. Remember to give your reasons (because …) when you write.

E Increase your wordpower (Talking about possibilities)

Grammar you can use
▶ 1.6

It is very helpful when you are discussing topics or expressing an opinion to be able to say how 'sure' or 'unsure' you are about things. The expressions in the box can all be used to do this. Use them to write sentences about the topics below, then compare your answers with a partner. (Note: if you are not clear about modal verbs like *may / might / could,* you can check them in the grammar summary.)

will (definitely)	**may well**	**may**	**might / could**
It is certain that … It is definite that … There is no doubt that… I am totally convinced that …	It is more or less certain that … It is very probable that … It is very likely that …	It is possible that … Maybe … Perhaps …	It is not likely that … It is not probable that… It is doubtful that … There is only a small chance that …
100 %	75 %	50 %	20 %-10 %

a Everyone in my class is on a social networking site like Facebook or MySpace.
b I'll meet my next boyfriend / girlfriend online.
c It is easier to talk to people online than in real life.
d The internet has improved all our lives.
e Girls are better at technology than boys.
f Some people are completely addicted to the internet.
g In 20 years it will be difficult to remember a world without the web.
h You can do everything on the internet.

2 Cyberbullying (Two personal stories)

You are going to listen to two American teenagers talking about problems they had online. The recordings are from the website of an organisation called Netsmartz which aims to teach students about the dangers of the internet.

CD 5, 6

Sound and (moving) images ▶ 1.2

A Understanding the texts

Listen to the two teenagers' stories and take notes. Then retell one of the stories in your own words to the class.

✕ **Extra:** Take one of the stories and write an account of what happened, pointing out how the boy or Amy felt afterwards and why.

B Analysing the texts

1. Read the introduction at the top of the page again. Define precisely in your own words the intentions of the Netsmartz organisation. Explain further why this organisation feels that this is so important.
2. Analyse the way the teenagers' stories get the message across. Consider the following questions. Remember in each case to point out why the makers of the recording made certain choices, and the effects of various techniques on the listener.
   a Who is the central character in each story? How old is he / she? How like the listeners?
   b Why is each story a first person narrative?
   c How would you characterise the stories (sad, amusing, ...)?
   d How are the stories structured?

C Reacting to the texts

Talk in class. Describe your personal reactions to the stories. Decide if what each teenager did was in some way 'stupid' - or can you understand their actions?

Written texts ▶ 5.2b

✕ **Extra:** Write an email to one of the teenagers giving your reactions to their online story.

3 Paying the price (A brochure)

You are going to read an extract from an Irish government brochure for teenagers. Then you will discuss the problem of giving too much information online.

A Understanding the brochure

Written texts ▸ 3.1

Read the extract then sum up in your own words the danger it highlights. Guess the unknown words from the context, using your dictionary only if necessary.

2020 Generation Z

Social networking sites (e.g. Bebo, Facebook, MySpace & Pizco) are a great place to catch up with friends and to meet new people. While many social networking sites allow users to restrict access, surveys have shown that the majority of users are not activating the privacy settings or safety measures. [...]

Revealing too much about yourself, your relationships and what you get up to in your spare time can have implications down the line - the past can creep up on you ...

Scenario

As you make postings and upload videos and photos onto your social networking site, unknown to you, an electronic 'spider' trawling the world wide web caches (saves) your pages. Even though you delete content on your pages every few months, to your horror a collection of videos, photos and postings created by you as a teenager resurface in the year 2020 in an archive on the net entitled 'Generation Z: the Lost Years'.

It is the year 2020 and you have an important interview for promotion coming up. You are counting on getting the promotion and the pay rise that comes with it in order to secure a mortgage on your first house. A former schoolmate alerts you to the Generation Z archive. You are worried that your employer will come across this material as part of its screening process. Some of the photos and conversations on record now come across as quite shocking.

[From: Office of the Data Protection Commissioner, Ireland]

B Discussing the problems

Work first in groups to collect ideas about the questions below, then talk in class.

a Did this extract surprise you? Why (not)?
b How well-informed do you feel you are generally about internet dangers?
c What have you learned about internet dangers (for example, at school or from reading magazines)? How helpful do you find the advice you got?
d Thinking of the other texts from this topic, what do you think is the biggest danger for teenagers from modern technologies like the internet or mobile phones? Why?

SEQUENCE

04

MAKING A BETTER WORLD

It is your world – you are the people who will live in it and shape it in the future. Unfortunately, there is much that is wrong. In this sequence, we look at some of the issues that face you and how young people are already trying to make a better world.

Collect ideas

1. Look at the pictures above and on the next page which illustrate some of the problems in the world today. What problems are illustrated? List the issues and give specific examples of such problems that you know about.

Sound and (moving) images ► 2

2. Look at the picture on the next page of a crowd of young people. Speculate about what is happening in this scene and list some words to describe the feelings of the people involved.

Activity chest ► 2

3. Brainstorm some ideas about other things that young people can do to make their voice heard and to try to build a better world. Think, for example, of:
   - what you as an individual can do in your everyday life to help with the problem of global warming,
   - what organisations you might join to get involved, people (media etc.) you might contact – or even speak to directly,
   - how you could organise an initiative in your own school or town,
   - what possibilities the internet offers,
   - how you could express your ideas creatively.
4. Work in groups.

Written texts ► 5.2

   a Make a mindmap about the issues facing today's world and the ways in which you could take action to try to improve the situations.
   b Prepare and give a talk: 'The future is in our hands'.

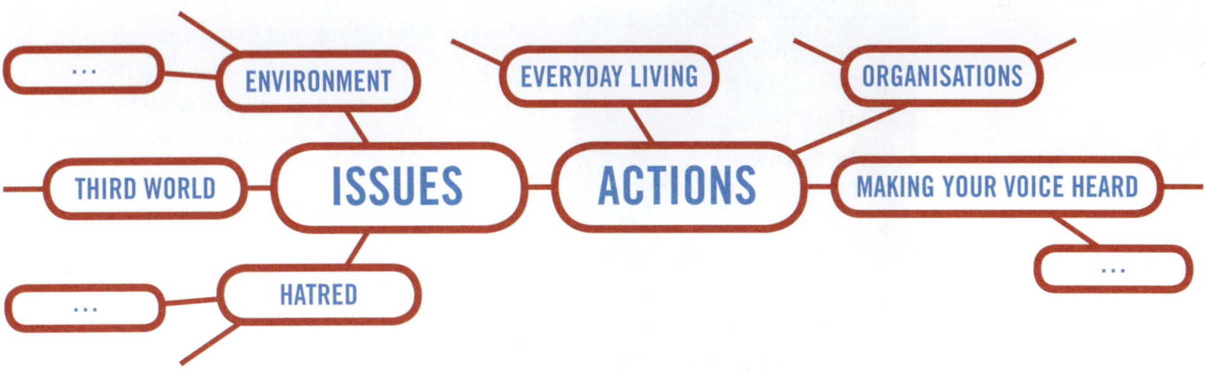

When you look around you at the world we live in, it is clear / obvious / evident / easy to see that ...	
there is much that is wrong / there are a great many problems that need to be solved.	
One of these is / Another is ... / One of the biggest crises facing the world today is ... / In many parts of the world there is (are) ... / Many people are (also) deeply concerned about ... / It is (also) tragic that ...	
It is up to us / young people like us / our generation	to bring about change / to tackle these problems / to play our part in creating a better world.
We must know about / be aware of / be informed about / not turn our backs on ...	
We can take action, too, by	demonstrating / writing to ... / ...

TOPIC 01

Young people getting involved

1 Young people and politics (A blog)

You are going to read a post from an Australian website for young people. The website is run by ActNow, an organisation that exists in Australia to inform teenagers and 20-somethings about important issues and to help them to get involved.

A Before you read

Activity chest ▶ 2

The writer of the post is going to define 'politics'. In groups, brainstorm the words and ideas that come into your mind when you hear the word 'politics', then tell the class.

Are young people political enough?

Are we politically active or apathetic, disengaged and ignorant?

Submitted by Josie Views 10637 Comments 6

In August 2006, I attended a seminar on the results of a study into young people and political engagement. The findings presented were interesting and somewhat contradictory. The study found that young people (that's us) tend to think politics is boring and removed from our everyday lives. But in contrast, most of us are interested in and concerned about a number of (political) issues. It appears that we tend to distinguish formal political structures and institutions (like parliament and voting) from less formal structures and participation (like petitions, protests, volunteering with organisations and issues) and, in general, we don't define the latter as 'political'.

I think the stereotype that young people are apathetic and disengaged in politics, stems from the way we define politics. Much of the research in this field takes a narrow view of politics and political participation, identifying it with formal structures and institutions. Since young people are less interested in these formal structures, academia, politicians and the popular press have too often assumed that young people are disengaged. Contrary to this view, I believe that young people are very much engaged in politics by their awareness and activism on social issues, from volunteering to debating and protesting.

Headline *apathetic:* not caring about anything
4 *contradictory:* widersprüchlich
7 *removed from sth.:* not relevant to sth.
10 *distinguish (A from B):* make a difference between (A and B)
13 *petition:* Bittbrief
16 *the latter:* the last one mentioned
18 *stem from sth.:* come from sth.
21 *academia:* professors etc. in universities

Are you interested in politics?

Whenever I pose this question to other young people like my friends and even to older people, I almost always get a cringe and a lecture about politics being uncool, full of corruption and completely irrelevant to our lives. But paradoxically, when we begin talking, our conversation is filled with political issues, whether it's multiculturalism, poverty in Africa, the war in the Middle East, the plight of refugees, terrorism, censorship or global warming. So I find that while most people claim at first to be uninterested in politics, they usually are more engaged than they realise. I think that that comes down to the way we define politics.

So what is 'politics'?

For me, politics is about the issues that affect people and the world around them. This means issues we are passionate about as well as more formal institutional structures, like government, parliament and voting. So multiculturalism, war, taxes, poverty, homelessness, long hospital waiting list, water restrictions, school funding etc, are all politics. So if you're interested in any of these issues, then you're interested in politics. [...]

[From: www.actnow.com © 2006 Josephine Khali]

27 *cringe:* peinliche Reaktion, Schaudern
27 *lecture:* Vortrag
28 *corruption:* dishonest, immoral behaviour
30 *plight:* bad situation
31 *censorship:* Zensur
37 *passionate:* having very strong feelings
39 *restrictions:* Einschränkungen

B Understanding the text

Sum up the views on young people's attitudes towards politics presented in the post.

In this text, the writer	compares / contrasts young people's attitudes towards … and … / makes a distinction between …
She claims / maintains / argues / puts forward the opinion that …	
She	supports this idea by … / backs this up with …
Her conclusion is (that) … / She comes to the conclusion that …	

C Analysing the text

Written texts ▶ 2.2b

Analyse how the writer tries to make clear to the reader her view on young people and politics. Take into account these points:
- the structure of the text,
- how and why she uses examples from her own experience,
- how she speaks to the reader (directly? indirectly? …?).

D Reacting to the text

Activity chest ▶ 14

In groups, hold 'Silent discussions' about the questions below.

a Has your definition of politics changed now? Why (not)?
b Could you imagine becoming politically engaged now? Why (not)?

2 Teen initiatives (Case studies)

The list of issues that young people can become involved in is so long that a good way to get a general picture is to look in detail at some specific examples or 'case studies'. The following web pages are from an American website, WKCD – What Kids Can Do.

Written texts
▶ 2.2c

A Before you read

List in class social or political issues that might interest young people locally, nationally or globally.

B Understanding the case studies

1. Look at the webpage below and sum up in your own words:
   - the context in which you read these case studies (the organisation, its purpose, how the web page is organised and why),
   - what the organisation itself says about the value of case studies.
2. Work in groups to study these two texts. For each text, make notes about the following points, then report to the class:
   - what kind of initiative is presented in the case study,
   - what aims it pursues,
   - what it does to achieve these aims,
   - how successful it has been so far,
   - who has joined the initiative and why.

Voices and work from the next generation

FEATURE STORIES NEXT GENERATION PRESS OTHER WKCD SITES

On this website, WKCD presents young people's lives, learning, and work, and their partnerships with adults both in and out of school. Our community of readers stretches from youth organizers in some of this country's toughest urban areas to policy makers at the national level. We believe that a good story well told crosses geographies, generations, class and race, and position.

New on our front page ...

Everyone Has a Story to Tell: The Faces of Homelessness

More ...

Bike it: How Students at One School Are Reducing Their Carbon Footprint

More ...

Case Study 1

EVERYONE HAS A STORY TO TELL: THE FACES OF HOMELESSNESS

by Barbara Cervone

ORLANDO, FL—The calculus of living paycheck to paycheck in America keeps getting harder. Pay the rent but drop the life-saving medication. Skip lunch so there's enough for dinner. Give up the phone but hold onto the car. We hear it often: many Americans are just one or two paychecks away from being homeless.

Nineteen-year-old Shardy Camargo in Orlando, Florida knows this well. She and her mother – who worked for more than ten years as a minimum-wage cashier at McDonald's – lost everything they had when Shardy was a high school freshman. After a failed try to find stability with relatives in the Dominican Republic, they joined the estimated two to three million homeless Americans who live day-to-day in shelters, cars, makeshift tents, or on the streets. Roughly 40 percent are families with minor children.

"Going into middle school, I didn't know we had financial problems," said Carmago. "I thought it was normal. My mother kept applying for food stamps and kept getting rejected because they said she made 'too much,' even though we were having to skip meals. Then, suddenly, even the little bit we'd built up went away."

When she and her mother got back on their feet, Carmago became a regular volunteer at Orlando's Coalition for the Homeless. At Maynard Evans High School, she joined the Beta Club, a national community-outreach program. With more than 45 classmates, she started what has become a multi-year project to tell the stories of Orlando's homeless—in print and video. [...]

The students decided to interview men and women at the city's homeless shelter, and Carmago's strong ties to the people living there provided remarkable access. The students interviewed 30 residents, wrote up their stories, and published them in a book. [...] Then, thanks to a grant from Disney, the Beta Club turned their passion and talents to creating a documentary video. As with the book, their goal was to punch through the stereotypes of the homeless – that they are uneducated, unmotivated, and unfit. They also wanted to feature the stories of youth who are homeless, like Shardy Carmago.

"For the film we went out looking for individuals who were willing to tell their story," explained senior Nickelle Smith, current president of the Beta Club. "There's a lake in Orlando that attracts a lot of homeless people and that's where we started."

"We were surprised how many people we asked actually wanted to be interviewed, to be part of the film," added Steev Bilius, a junior. "They saw it as a chance to have their voices heard. They sensed the impact their words and stories would have."

Over the course of six months, the students took the video from start to finish: creating a storyboard, finding folks to interview, then filming their interviews, editing, selecting music, and creating graphics. The results are extraordinary. The film is professional in every sense, and the stories of the nine homeless individuals that fill these 32 minutes are breathtaking in their honesty and strength. [...]

1 *calculus:* (here) the need to work out sth. mathematically
2 *skip sth.:* not have sth.
8 *cashier:* Kassiererin
9 *freshman (AE):* first year student
9 *stability:* safe, regular life
11 *shelter:* Obdachlosenasyl
12 *minor:* under 16
13 *middle school (AE):* school for pupils of about ages 9-14
14 *food stamp:* paper from government to buy cheap food
15 *reject sb./sth.:* jdn./etwas ablehnen
15 *make sth.:* (here) earn sth.
20 *community-outreach:* Öffentlichkeitsarbeit
21 *multi-year:* lasting a number of years
24 *tie:* relationship, contact
28 *punch through sth.:* go beyond sth.
32 *senior (AE):* student in last years of high school
37 *impact:* effect
40 *storyboard:* Ablaufplan (eines Filmes)

46 *misconception:* wrong idea
52 *patch:* short period
55 *Herculean:* almost impossible
56 *enrollment:* number of people who joined
56 *gather steam:* in Gang kommen
57 *evidence:* Beweis
59 *affirmation:* Bestätigung
61 *feature sth.:* (here) etwas enthalten
63 *relentless:* unnachgiebig
63 *unwavering:* standhaft
63 *commitment:* Engagement
64 *tenth grader:* Zehntklässer
64 *recall sth.:* remember sth.
66 *coin:* Münze
66 *change:* 1 Kleingeld, 2 Änderung

For Beta Club members Nickelle and Steev, the impact of their work feels substantial. "Going into it," said Steev, "I had the standardized misconceptions about homeless people, like they're uneducated or lazy. I learned that 'homeless' isn't a title, it's human beings that deserve the respect and support all people deserve." Students across Orlando County who have seen the film are getting that message, these young documentarians believe.

"It's opened students' eyes to the humanity we all share," said Nickelle. "For me and my mom, it reminded us how we, too, could hit a patch of bad luck and find ourselves in a shelter." What the homeless need most are jobs, these students concluded. When a person without savings loses a job, re-entering the labor market can prove a Herculean task.

Enrollment in the club doubled as the project gathered steam. "It's evidence," said Jennifer Bohn (the teacher at Maynard Evans High who helps run the Beta Club), "that students want to be part of the solution." And the homeless people they interviewed reported feeling affirmation, despite the loss and mistakes that filled their stories. Soon, the students will publish a new book, Grow Where You Are Planted, featuring poems by youth about their experiences with homelessness.

"These kids are relentless, passionate, unwavering in their commitment to their community and to service," said Bohn. One tenth grader, she recalled, told her, "Ms. Bohn, I just realized something. Homeless people don't want coins, they want change."

Case Study 2

BIKE IT: HOW STUDENTS AT ONE CALIFORNIA HIGH SCHOOL ARE REDUCING THEIR CARBON FOOTPRINT

Founded in 2004, the Samohi Solar Alliance (SSA) is a student-run, grassroots organization working to inspire environmental awareness, education, and tangible change at Santa Monica High School (Samohi) and in the greater community. […]

Recently, WKCD spoke with Lulu Mickelson, Samohi senior and co-president of SSA, about the Alliance's many accomplishments, including the 'Bike It' initiative.

3 *tangible:* easy to see and touch
7 *accomplishment:* Leistung
9 *solarize sth.:* adapt sth. to use solar power
10 *district:* Bezirk (-sregierung)
11 *tap into sth.:* make use of sth.
12 *funds:* Finanzmittel
12 *allocate sth.:* etwas bereitstellen
17 *settle on sth.:* choose sth.
18 *emit sth.:* etwas ausstoßen
20 *behavioral shift:* changes in the way people behave

Our first project, the initial reason SSA was created, was to solarize the school's swimming pool. After developing a game plan with the district, we helped raise the money for the initial testing of the roof and then we tapped into funds the district had allocated for structural redevelopment to cover the cost of the panels. […]

With these strategic victories, we decided to rethink what we were doing as a club, to move beyond solar panels and buildings. What do we do now? What's next? We decided to turn toward student behaviors that affect the school's carbon footprint. That's how we settled on transportation. We realized that reducing the CO_2 that was emitted from the cars that brought 3,050 students to and from school each day would be one of the easiest and most substantial ways we could make change, through behavioral shifts on campus.

Bike It

We started 'Bike Day', which has now escalated into the 'Bike It' initiative. We're trying to convince students to get to school without a car. Three to five days a year, we organize events that challenge students to find a new way to get to school, any way that doesn't involve a car–walking, biking, skateboarding, taking the bus. We do it on a day when there's staff development and school starts a little later, so there's no whining about having to get up earlier. It has become a big celebratory event on campus, everyone knows about it, everyone wants to participate. Students and staff who ditch their cars get a free popsicle; there are also raffles, lunchtime music and dancing, bike shops on campus, and student performers. Our hope, our idea is that when kids do it once, they will see how easy it is to go without a car and a long-term change is introduced.

We've had a lot of success. When I first started at Samohi, there were about 20 bikes a day on the racks. This year there's an average of 100 At this October's event, over 1,200 kids–40 percent of the students–used alternative transportation to get to school. At this next 'Bike It' day, we're aiming for 50 percent. On an ordinary day, about 80 percent of Samohi students come to school by car. [...]

Creating a movement

We know with our 'Bike It' initiative, half the battle is fighting against the car culture, which is huge in Los Angeles. People want to do what's most convenient, and for students, school is like a full-time job. They feel they are working so hard, they don't want the extra burden of having to ride their bike to school. Little do they know that when you ride your bike to school in the morning, you're actually more awake, you feel better–there are so many benefits health-wise, environment-wise, traffic-wise. I live two miles away from school and it takes me only five minutes more to bike to school.

Fortunately, being green, wearing green, thinking green has become cool. It's gone mainstream. There's an eco-chic fad, which I think is good if it goes beyond just a fad. I think the awareness is powerful. Now it is just about getting people to act on it.

[From: WhatKidsCanDo© Barbara Cervone]

22 *escalate:* grow fast
24 *challenge sb.:* jdn. herausfordern
26 *staff development:* Lehrerfortbildung
27 *whine:* jammern
28 *celebratory:* feierlich
29 *ditch sth.:* (here) not use sth.
30 *popsicle (AE):* Eis am Stiel
30 *raffle:* Gewinnspiel
35 *(bicycle) rack:* (here) Fahrradständer
42 *huge:* extremely important
43 *convenient:* easy to do
44 *burden:* Belastung
50 *go mainstream:* become popular
50 *fad:* short-lived fashion
52 *act on sth.:* nach etwas handeln

C Analysing the case studies

Written texts ► 2.2c

Work in groups to collect your ideas about the two case studies.

a What is a 'case study'? Why are case studies often written?

b Explain why these two texts are case studies. Point out clearly, with examples, how they illustrate the two key aspects of a case study: 'specific' and 'general'.

D Reacting to the case studies

Activity chest ► 12

1. Would you support either of these initiatives? Justify your answer.
2. Think of an initiative that would be worth starting at your school. Work in groups with 'Placemats' to collect ideas and present them to the class.

3 BUNDjugend (Mediation)

An English-speaking friend who is visiting you in Germany is interested in environmental issues. You are looking together at this web page. Give your friend the most important information in English.

Bund für Umwelt und Naturschutz Deutschland

BUND

FREUNDE DER ERDE

BUND.net > Über uns > BUNDjugend

... und jetzt noch die Erde retten!

Es geht um unsere Zukunft

... und die nehmen wir selbst in die Hand. Denn schließlich ist es unsere Welt, in der wir leben und die wir verändern können.

Die **BUNDjugend** ist eine umweltpolitische Jugendorganisation, die sich mit Worten und Taten für Alternativen einsetzt und mit ihren Forderungen Denkprozesse anregt. Wir sind nicht nur in den einzelnen Bundesländern, sondern deutschlandweit aktiv und durch unser Netzwerk „Young Friends of the Earth" mit Jugendlichen aus der ganzen Welt verbunden.

Unser Ziel?

... die Erde retten. Die **BUNDjugend** setzt sich erfolgreich und öffentlichkeitswirksam in Kampagnen, Protestaktionen und Projekten für die Umwelt ein. Wir kämpfen für gentechnikfreies Essen, eine giftfreie Umwelt, machen uns stark für die Erhaltung der Natur, für eine gerechte Globalisierung und für 100 Prozent erneuerbare Energien. Wir glauben an eine positive Zukunft, die wir durch unseren Einsatz und unser Engagement mitgestalten und bestimmen können.

Die Welt verändert sich, aber die Richtung können wir bestimmen. Bei uns ist Platz für Meinungen und kreative Ideen. Wir stellen Projekte und Aktionen auf die Beine. Bei uns übernehmen junge Menschen Verantwortung und bestimmen unsere Themen und Inhalte mit.

Du kannst etwas bewegen

... und die **BUNDjugend** bietet dir die ideale Umgebung, egal ob du mit deinem Engagement erst anfängst oder schon erfahren bist: Bei uns kannst du aktiv werden. In vielen lokalen und bundesweiten Arbeitskreisen zum Thema Globaliserung, Konsum, Umweltbildung und zu erneuerbaren Energien kannst du mit diskutieren, Projekte und Aktionen umsetzen oder du rüttelst mit erfolgreicher Pressearbeit unsere PolitikerInnen kräftig wach. Zusätzlich bieten wir dir inhaltliche und methodische Workshops und Seminare an, wie „Richtig Argumentieren", AD-Busting und andere kreative Protestformen, Stadtführung, Zeitmanagement und vieles mehr.

[From: Bund für Umwelt und Naturschutz Deutschland e.V.]

Grammar you can use
▶ 1.5
Answers
▶ pp. 172

A Check your grammar (Conditional sentences)

1. The sentences below could be used to talk about 'making a better world'. They are all examples of conditional sentences 1, 2 or 3. Complete each sentence with the correct form of the verb.

a If we do nothing about global warming, it ***will get*** (get) worse.
b If we shared out all the food in the world, everyone … (have) enough to eat.
c I … (join) the BUNDjugend organisation if I had known about it before.
d If there … (be) fewer cars on the roads, the air would be much cleaner.
e The family wouldn't have become homeless if the mother … (not / lose) her job.
f If you … (get) involved personally, you will find that 'politics' is actually quite interesting.
g I think lots of people … (be) interested if you made a film about this topic.
h If people 100 years ago … (know) about global warming, maybe they … (behave) differently.

2. You have to write a short text entitled: 'If I had an unlimited amount of money to change the world'. Write five sentences using conditional 2. Use different verbs.
If I had all that money, first, I …
I … also … if I didn't have to worry about the cost.
…

B Increase your wordpower (Words to describe emotions)

1. Group the words in the box into 'positive' and 'negative', then use them to complete the sentences below. More than one word is possible.

angry – anxious – apathetic – apprehensive – calm – cheerful – concerned – cynical – depressed – disappointed – disillusioned – enthusiastic – fanatical – gloomy – hopeful – indifferent – irritated – keen – loving – negative – optimistic – passionate – pessimistic – positive – sad – worried

POSITIVE	NEGATIVE
calm	*angry*
…	…

a Many people feel ***passionate*** about politics.
b Generally speaking, I feel … about our chances to make a better world.
c I think we all have to be … when we think about the world's problems.
d So how do you feel about this? – To tell you the truth, I am totally …
e It is hard not to be … when you watch TV news programmes.
f Whenever I see pictures like these of starving children, I feel …

2. Write more sentences of your own using the words in the box.

TOPIC 02

Getting to the truth

As a consumer, you think about the price before you buy something. But what else may be important? Also, you are surrounded by adverts, which tell you how to spend your money. But what else do you expect from adverts you see around you? How 'honest' are they?

Collect ideas

1. Make a list of ten things you and your family buy. Then consider what criteria you use to choose them – their quality? their impact on the environment? where and how they were made? … ? Give examples to illustrate your ideas.
2. When and why do you look at advertisements? What do you want an advertisement to tell you about a product or service? What is a 'bad' advertisement in your opinion? Give an example.

1 GM foods (An educational video and an e-zine article)

The chances are that you already eat GM (genetically modified) foods. Growing certain GM crops (at the moment chiefly maize) is allowed in most EU countries, but genetically modified foods, such as soya, are regularly imported from outside the EU. However, many environmentalists are worried about genetic modification and see in it a number of dangers.
So what is it exactly that you, a consumer, may be eating, and should you be worried? What is the 'truth' about GM?

A Before you begin

Activity chest ► 4

Give an oral summary of the main points of the following text.

a GM means 'changing things in nature'. Who first did this scientifically and how? How did his work help others?

b How did the discovery of DNA enable scientists to change things in new ways?

c How quickly did GM foods follow on from this discovery? What do you imagine the reason for this is?

A short history of GM

Gregor Mendel

Although he knew nothing about 'genes' as we understand them today, Gregor Mendel is considered to be the 'father of modern genetics'. Mendel (1822-1884) was an Austrian monk. After studying at university, Mendel experimented with peas in the garden of the monastery where he lived. His interest was in how the characteristics of different plants passed from one generation of peas to the next and he discovered that there were certain laws about how this happened. The practical use of Mendel's work was that it allowed growers and farmers to improve their crops. By selecting certain plants for growing, characteristics such as stronger growth and sweeter peas could be encouraged. This process is known as 'selective breeding'.

15 *selective breeding:* Auslesezüchtung

DNA

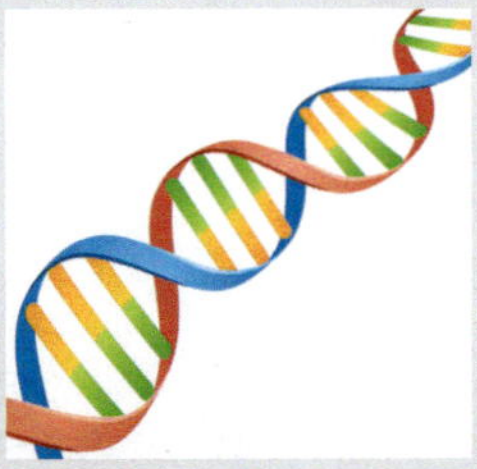

A computer model of DNA

DNA (deoxyribonucleic acid) is the substance that contains all the information that every living thing needs in order to grow. Many different scientists played a part in its discovery, but it was two British scientists, James Watson and Francis Crick, who first described fully the famous 'double helix' and so explained its structure. DNA contains the genes which, generally speaking, are each responsible for one piece of information. In the 1980s, scientists began to draw maps of the DNA structures of various plants and animals (including humans) so that they had a clear picture of which genes did what.

Genetic modification

The basic idea of genetic modification is very simple: by taking genes from one plant or animal and putting them into another, the characteristics of the first can be transferred to the second. Alternatively, it is possible to 'turn off' a gene in a plant or animal and so remove a characteristic. Both of these processes change ('modify') an existing plant or animal. Tomatoes were the very first genetically modified food plants, which began to be produced in the early 1990s.

DVD 12

1. GM in action: an educational video

B Understanding the video

You are going to watch a British television programme for secondary schools. Take notes in a chart like the one below. Compare with a partner, then write a summary of what you learned from the video.

FIRST TWO SCIENTISTS:		
Modified foods - *bananas* - …	How?	Why?
SCIENTIST AT THE END:		
GM in laboratory - …	GM outside a laboratory - …	

Notes on the video
herb: Kraut
Syngenta: company that develops GM foods
antifungal: antipilz-
onion: Zwiebel
radish: Radieschen
poisonous: giftig
toxic: giftig
salmon: Lachs
threefold: dreifach
meddle with sth.: etwas herumdoktern
haphazard: willkürlich
release sth.: etwas freisetzen

C Reacting to the video

Remembering that this video was made for schools, evaluate the view it gives of GM (positive? negative? biased?). Justify your answer.

[From: ITN Source/ECL]

2. GM in action: an e-zine article

The article you are going to read is from an e-zine called Teen Ink. This internet magazine, started in 1989 in the USA, is special because it is run by teenagers for teenagers. Any young person can send in articles about topics that interest them - poems, stories, and much more.

GENETICALLY MODIFIED FOODS: DISASTER OR DELIGHT?

By Mickie..., Hamilton, Canada

NORTH AMERICA. The continent we call home. With its majestic mountains, magnificent fresh water lakes and abundance of agricultural land, there is plenty to love about home. In fact, we tend to pride ourselves on the natural, locally grown products available within our borders. The farming trade has been part of the American way of life for hundreds of years. Recently though, there was a major change that altered the way food was to be grown not only in America, but all over the world.

It was the hot topic on TV; everybody had something to add to the discussion. Some were outraged, others overjoyed. What could possibly have caused such an uproar within our society? Genetically modified food, that's what. Now, the concept of genetically modifying something is not new in and of itself. But never have we been able to take a gene from one animal or plant and integrate it into another (animal or plant) until very recently. You see, in the year 1996, GM foods were officially widely available and used in a number of everyday products, from breakfast cereals and cooking oils to soda pop. Nobody had much to say about it, because nobody really knew. Farmers had slowly been switching over to this new and exciting way of cultivating. Why? The answer is obvious. Marketers promised the moon with these new seeds. Pesticides would no longer be needed, and the health issues that came along with them would be eliminated. Produce would stay fresher, longer, AND be able to better withstand frost. Plus there would be more food, which could be sent overseas to countries that were suffering from famine. All thanks to genetic modification. Guess what? These were not empty promises. The new crops really were that fantastic. The genetic engineers behind this revolution made it plain that they could accomplish even more with this technology. For instance, removing the allergy gene from a peanut, making it safe for millions with that allergy. Scientists felt the world was at their fingertips, what could possibly go wrong?

Well, when American consumers did find out that so much of what they ate had been genetically altered in some way, the consensus was either one of anger or confusion. They were angry because of being kept in a state of ignorance on such an important and personal issue. People were worried about the possible side effects as well. Scientists that were against this development, argued that GM foods could be causing severe allergic reactions for some, since they were injecting proteins into foods that humans have never consumed before. For instance they injected a strawberry with a fish gene, causing the fruit to be able to withstand frost better.

Headline *delight:* Wonne
1 *majestic:* beeindruckend
2 *abundance:* Fülle
3 *pride ourselves on sth.:* be proud of sth.
9 *outraged:* angry
9 *overjoyed:* very happy
10 *uproar:* Aufruhr
11 *in and of itself:* an sich
15 *soda pop:* lemonade
16 *switch:* change
17 *obvious:* easy to see
18 *seed:* Saatkorn
18 *pesticide:* Pflanzenschutzmittel
19 *eliminate sth.:* end sth., take sth. away
20 *withstand sth.:* eine Sache widerstehen
24 *plain:* clear
26 *be at one's fingertips:* vollständig beherrschbar
29 *consensus:* general opinion
32 *side effect:* Nebenwirkung
34 *inject sth.:* etwas inizieren

Plus there was no concrete way of proving that the new foods were safe or unsafe. Also genetic modification has affected exporting in North America. Other countries will not accept products that contain the slightest trace of GM food. The fact that nothing was labelled as being a GM product was another big cause for upset. People got scared and began to panic, and rightly so. If something contains by-products, then the label has to say so, because they know that some consumers abstain from foods containing blood. If it contains dairy, then they list it in the ingredients knowing that some people are allergic. But for some reason GM foods had no advance warning supplied. The consumer's rights were not being respected.

There is definitely a lot of good and bad that seems to derive from this topic. My opinion though, is that GM foods should be a CHOICE for us, but only a choice. Science has made some amazing leaps through genetic modification that I think will prove to be good for us as time goes on. Plus I have been exposed to GM foods my entire life. Eating them has been a daily occurrence. Maybe it would be a different story if I had never been exposed to this kind of product. But [...] there has not been any major side effect that I am aware of. I am healthy and do not feel that GM foods have restricted my abilities at all. Nevertheless, as stated beforehand, there should always be a choice. If GM foods are to stay on the market they must be labelled so that consumers can decide for themselves what they want to be putting into their mouths and their families' mouths. It is a right, not a luxury. Plus it would be extremely helpful if the government would launch a campaign, giving the people an unbiased explanation of both sides of the story, equipping us with the skills and knowledge that we need in order to make an informed decision for ourselves. Through my eyes, this is the best way to continue the exploration that has lead humans to such amazing heights without hurting anyone in the process.

So, there is plenty of good that has come from genetically modified foods. And there is some bad that is suspected to arise with time. The subject has certainly gotten its fair share of media coverage. But in the end, it is all about the choice you make for yourself and the food you decide to purchase. Make it fair; give GM foods a chance while keeping good old natural products in the grocery stores.

[From: www.teenink.com]

39 *slight:* very small
trace: Spur
40 *label sth.:* etwas etikettieren, kennzeichnen
41 *upset:* worry
43 *abstain from sth.:* (here) not eat sth.
43 *dairy:* Molkereiprodukt
44 *ingredient:* Zutat
45 *advance warning:* Vorwarnung
45 *supply sth.:* etwas bereitstellen
47 *derive from sth.:* come from sth.
49 *leap:* Sprung
50 *be exposed to sth.:* be in contact with
51 *occurrence:* event
52 *be exposed to sth.:* einer Sache ausgesetzt sein
54 *restrict sth.:* limit sth.
60 *equip sb. with sth.:* jdn. mit etwas ausrüsten
65 *suspect sth.:* etwas ahnen
67 *purchase sth.:* buy sth.
68 *good old:* known and loved

D Understanding the article

1. Pick out the main points of the article in the following way:
   a Outline the impact that GM foods had in North America when they were first introduced there – giving any necessary historical background.
   b List the arguments for and against the new foods.
   c Sum up Mickie's personal view of GM and her reasons.
   d Summarise her personal message to her readers at the end.
2. Write answers to the questions.
   a Outline the role of GM crops in North American life according to the writer and her personal opinion about the issue.
   b Say how and why the writer thinks young people should react to GM crops.

Activity chest
► 12

E Analysing the article

Work in groups using a 'Placemat' to collect your ideas about the tasks below then prepare and give a report to the class.

Working in groups and on projects
► 1

1. Classify the text as one of the four main types of non-fictional texts and give briefly your reasons.
2. Sum up the writer's intentions and explain how she attempts to achieve her goals. Consider the following points:
   - how personally written her article is (give examples and point out the personal pronouns she uses) and why she chooses to write this way,
   - how she refers to an image of North America and the effect this has on her readers,
   - the way she structures the article generally and her reasons for this,
   - how she highlights the importance of the issue of GM crops and why she does this.

F Reacting to the article and finding out more about GM

Written texts
► 5.1

1. Express your views about Mickie's article in class. How do you feel about her decision to write the article? Do you believe that articles like this can actually change things? Why (not)? Has the article helped you to understand the issue better? Why (not)?
2. Like all new sciences, GM causes enormous controversy. For some, it promises a better world in which we can feed starving children and grow crops that resist pests, taste better, and are healthier. For others, however, GM crops and animals are 'Frankenstein foods' – unnatural, potentially dangerous, and in no way the solution to the world's food problems.

Working in groups and on projects
► 3,4

Organise a class project to find out more. In groups, go online to gather information – for example, from a large producer of GM crops like the American company Monsanto and from environmental organisations such as Greenpeace or Friends of the Earth. Make group presentations of your findings in class, then discuss the arguments as a whole. Finally, make a poster that sums up your personal view and present it to the class.

2 Presenting a green image (Advertisements)

We expect advertisments to be truthful and honest even when they are trying to persuade us to buy something. But in a world where businesses want to appear 'green', how sure can we be that advertising is really giving us the whole truth? (Note: although some names have been changed or left out, all the advertisements that follow are based on real examples.)

A Before you begin

a What aspects of a product or industry could be 'green'? (How and where things are made / the materials used / transport ...)

b Do you agree that companies and industries nowadays want to 'appear green'? Which of these may worry particularly about their image? Why?

B Analysing an advertisement

Written texts
▶ 2.2a

Work in groups to collect your ideas about this advertisement, then report to the class. Consider the following aspects:

a What image of SUVs (Sports Utility Vehicles) is presented in the ad? Describe in detail how this image is conveyed to a consumer.

b What do you know about this type of car? (Fuel consumption? Impact on the environment? ...)

c When an advertisement tries to give a green image to a product which is not naturally green, it is called 'greenwashing'. Explain why (or why not) you think this ad could be an example of greenwashing.

C Analysing more advertisements

In your groups, look in detail at the advertisements on the next page. For one advertisement there are some notes to help you. For each ad, take into account the following points:

a What are the 'facts' as far as you know them about what is being advertised, particularly with regard to issues such as the environment, health or the protection of wild animals?

b How does the advertisement attempt to create an image of what is being advertised which is greener than it may be in reality? Does it:
- 'tell lies' about a product?
- use a strange 'logic' in its argument?
- give information that is true, but is not the 'whole truth'?
- give information that is true, but actually completely irrelevant?
- use colour / people / images etc. to put across its message? How?

trapper: Pelzjäger
vital: lebenswichtig
habitat: Lebensraum
regulated: (gesetzlich) geregelt
conservation authorities: Naturschutzbehörde

Note:
The picture above is from a TV commercial by one of Europe's largest energy producers. The ad featured the 'Energieriese'. At the time, 2 % of the company's energy came from windpower (or other renewable sources), 98 % from coal-fired power stations.

D Reacting to the advertisements

Talk in class. How aware were you before of 'greenwashing'? What are your reactions now to ads like these? Is greenwashing an important issue? Why (not)?

✕ **Extra:** Go online and collect more examples of greenwashing and present them to the class. Just google: 'greenwashing examples'.

3 Who can you trust? (Ecolabels)

A Der blaue Engel **B** EU Ecolabel **C** Energy Star

D Fairtrade **E Leaping Bunny** **F Rainforest Alliance**

harm sth./sb.: jdm./etwas Leid zufügen
exploit: sb./sth.: jdn./etwas ausbeuten, ausnutzen

Consumers today want to know that what they buy is good for the environment, and that people and animals have not been harmed or exploited in the production of goods. So how can they know this? One way is to look for ecolabels. There are many of these. You can see some examples above.

Working in groups and on projects
▶ 3,4

A Researching and presenting an ecolabel

Organise groups in your class to find out about the labels and the organisations behind them, then make a presentation of your findings to the class. Use the grid below to collect information.

LABEL	*Der blaue Engel*
STARTED WHERE / WHEN / BY WHOM?	
COUNTRY / COUNTRIES WHERE USED?	
PRODUCTS COVERED BY LABEL?	
AIMS OF THE ORGANISATION BEHIND THE LABEL?	
SPECIAL FEATURES / INTERESTING FACTS?	

B Talk in class

How different or how similar are the labels you learned about? Which of the aspects of the different labels would you personally be most interested in? If you could invent a new label, what would it be? Design it and show the class.

TOPIC

03

Making your voice heard

The power of the human voice – spoken or written – is immense. Words can echo around the world, especially in the internet age, when a speech, a poem, a song or an article can reach millions almost immediately.

Collect ideas

Imagine that you could speak to the world's politicians at a big international conference (or publish an article or a poem – or sing a song) that would express an idea that is very important to you personally on the subject of 'making a better world'.

1. The pictures above suggest a few themes you might choose.. Work in groups to list the key words associated with each of the pictures. Here are some ideas:

poverty – street children – homelessness – destruction of the world's rainforests …

2. Which of the themes would you speak or write about? Is there another theme that is more important to you? Tell the class and mention a few of the key points you would want to convey to people around the world.

1 Six minutes that stopped the world (A speech)

In June 1992, over 100 world leaders and several thousand representatives of world organisations attended the Earth Summit conference organised by the United Nations in Rio de Janeiro, Brazil. The theme was the future of the environment worldwide. It was at this conference that a 12-year-old girl from Canada named Severn Suzuki made a speech that came to be known as 'six minutes that stopped the world'. You are going to listen to Severn's speech.

summit: Gipfeltreffen

A Before you listen

Consider why Severn's speech was so unusual.
- Describe as you imagine it the setting of the speech – where? who? why?
- Compare Severn with the people in the audience and the kinds of speakers that usually give speeches at such a conference.
- Speculate about Severn's feelings before, during and after her speech.
- Imagine and describe the emotions of her listeners during the speech.

CD 7, 8

B Understanding the speech

Sound and (moving) images ▶ 1.2

1. Listen to the speech once. Sum up what Severn expects adults to do. Compare with a partner and tell the class your idea.
2. Listen to the speech again in sections (CD 8). Take notes, then answer the questions below on each section.

Section 1	Sum up in your own words who Severn is, how she came to Brazil, and her reason for being there.
Section 2	Outline who Severn is fighting for and why.
Section 3	State how Severn characterises the people at the conference, and what she asks them to do about the problems she lists.
Section 4	Summarise what Severn tells her listeners in this section about the people she has met in the last two days, and the conclusions she has drawn from this meeting.
Section 5	Contrast the behaviour of children and adults as Severn characterises them in this section. Then sum up her final message to her listeners.

Written texts
▶ 2.2i

C Analysing the speech

You are going to analyse how Severn tries to convince her listeners that action must be taken immediately over the world's problems that she is concerned about.

1. Divide the class into groups to study the aspects below. (A group can study just one aspect, or it can look at several aspects). Listen to Severn's speech again, take notes, then use 'Placemats' to collect your ideas and report to the class.
   a **Severn the 12-year-old speaker**
   Identify the specific arguments that Severn uses as a child to appeal to her adult audience.
   b **A personal, emotional speech**
   Analyse how Severn makes her speech both personal and emotional in order to move her listeners and encourage them to act now. Explain the effect of her way of speaking on the audience.
   c **Rhetorical devices**
   Pick out and explain the effect of the rhetorical devices that Severn uses to stress her most important ideas and to drive her message home to the audience. Consider especially devices such as repetition and rhetorical questions.

Written texts
▶ 4.2

2. Speeches are often remembered for certain phrases that 'stick in the mind'. Listen to Severn's speech one last time and note down a phrase that you find particularly memorable. Put up some large sheets of paper in your classroom and write your phrase on one of them. Is there one phrase that has stuck in most of the students' minds? Can you explain why it is so memorable?

D Reacting to the speech

1. Severn's speech was described as 'six minutes that stopped the world'. Evaluate the speech yourself: is this a good description of it in your opinion? List the words you would use to describe it.
2. Severn gave her speech in 1992. Working in groups, list:
   a any problems that Severn mentioned then, which you feel could still be problems today,
   b any new problems that you feel have arisen in the world since her speech.
   What conclusions would you draw from your lists?
3. Plan and make a speech about another topic that is important to you. Use Severn's speech as a source of ideas for rhetorical devices, memorable phrases etc. You can only speak for five minutes. Use 'Peer review' to check and improve your speech.

Activity chest
▶ 11

Written texts
▶ 5.2e

2 Dreams (A song and four poems)

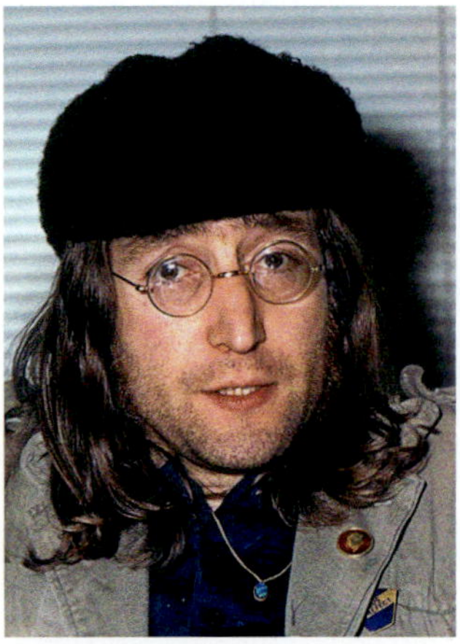

John Lennon (1940-80)

Martin Luther King Jr (1929-68)

It has often been said that 'the pen is mightier than the sword'. Writing poems and singing songs are powerful ways to make your voice heard – even for young people. And if you are a world-famous musician like John Lennon in the 1960s and 70s, your voice can reach millions. You are going to study a song text by John Lennon and four poems by a range of people, from young to old. Some of the poems were inspired by another famous speech: Martin Luther King's 'I have a dream'. All of them, however, touch on the theme of dreams.

1. 'Imagine' by John Lennon

Imagine there's no Heaven
It's easy if you try
No hell below us
Above us only sky
Imagine all the people
Living for today

Imagine there's no countries
It isn't hard to do
Nothing to kill or die for
And no religion too
Imagine all the people
Living life in peace

You may say that I'm a dreamer
But I'm not the only one
I hope someday you'll join us
And the world will be as one

Imagine no possessions
I wonder if you can
No need for greed or hunger
A brotherhood of man
Imagine all the people
Sharing all the world

You may say that I'm a dreamer
But I'm not the only one
I hope someday you'll join us
And the world will live as one

A Understanding the song

Work in groups using a 'Placemat' to answer the questions below.

a John Lennon was an atheist – he did not believe in God. In fact, he believed that religion had a harmful effect on society. In what two ways would the world be better without religion according to Lennon?

b Lennon deals with other themes in the song, too. Sum up what they are.

c What is Lennon's message to his listeners in the chorus of the song?

d Sum up what Lennon wants his listeners to do. Take into account the title of the song.

B Analysing the song

Written texts
▶ 2.3c

'Lennon aimed to make a better world with this song.' Analyse how he sets about doing this. Take into account the following points:

a How does he address his listeners and how does he try to involve them in his plans and dreams?

b Lennon was an expert song writer. Look at how he uses the conventions of songs to get across his message and how these devices affect the listener. Consider:
- the division into chorus / verses,
- the rhyme scheme,
- the repetition of key phrases and sentence patterns.

2. Four poems

Working in groups and on projects
▶ 1

Written texts
▶ 4.2

On the next page there are a number of poems, with notes about the people who wrote them. Divide the class into groups to look at one poem each, then present the poem to the class. (If you have time, your group can study a second or even third poem, too). Look at the following aspects of each poem:

a (Understanding the poem) Sum up its main theme.

b (Analysing the poem) Point out how it uses structure, rhetorical devices, images and any other features to convey its message.

C Reacting to the song and the poems

1. The song and the poems you have talked about are by a variety of writers, from the very young to a world-famous singer-songwriter. Which did you personally find most effective and why? (Skill in writing? Personally moving? Themes touched on? ...?) How did you react to John Lennon's ideas on religion?

Activity chest
▶ 11

Written texts
▶ 5.2e

2. Choose one of the formats (song text or poetic form) and write your own song or poem. Use 'Peer review' groups afterwards to compare, check and improve your texts.

Written texts
▶ 5.2a

3. In groups, talk about 'dreams'. What do dreams mean for you? What themes appear in your dreams? Why do people dream generally? Why are dreams such a powerful symbol of hope? Make a mindmap and show it to the class.

I have a dream

I have a dream that all people will be treated equally.

I have a dream that people would lay down their differences and be friends.

I have a dream that people will respect themselves and others.

I have a dream hunger will end and that peace will begin.

I have a dream that my dreams will become your dreams too.

I have a dream.

Trey

I have a dream

I have a dream that grown men will stop beating on our mothers.

I have a dream that people will stomp out tobacco and all of them get jobs.

I have a dream that people will stop killing or hurting each other.

I have a dream that it won't be prejudice in schools, neighborhoods, jobs, and out in the streets.

I have a dream that they will stop child abuse.

Those are my dreams. I want everyone to get in the habit of doing or believing in their dream. I hope these dreams will take over the world.

Taven

I have a dream

I had a dream last night
That racism would stop
White and black would become one

I had a dream last night
That terrorism would stop
Terrorists would just go away

I had a dream last night
That there would be peace in the world
The world would be perfect

Then I woke up
How I wish dreams were real

Sam

Dreams

Hold fast to dreams
For if dreams die
Life is a broken-winged bird
That cannot fly.
Hold fast to dreams
For when dreams go
Life is a barren field
Frozen with snow.

Langston Hughes

Top right
2 *beat on sb. (AE):* hit sb.
3 *stomp out:* (here) stop others (smoking)
8 *prejudice:* Vorurteil
11 *child abuse:* Kindesmisshandlung
Bottom right
7 *barren:* unfruchtbar

Notes on the poets on this page:

- **Trey** and **Taven** are 5th grade Delmar Elementary School pupils from Maryland, USA. Grade 5 students are usually around 10 years old.
- **Sam** is a grade 9 pupil at the Benjamin Britten High School in Lowestoft, England. Grade 9 pupils are usually around 15 years old.
- **Langston Hughes** (1902-1967) was an influential African-American poet, novelist, playwright and journalist.

TOPIC 04

Save the world, me?

For many people, global warming is the most serious threat we face today. But what can one individual person do to help? The answer is to reduce your 'carbon footprint' – to do everything you can to contribute less to the production of CO2 gases.

Collect ideas

Work in groups to make notes about the following points, then share your ideas in class.

a What is 'global warming' and what are some of the things that cause it?

b What effects of global warming have you heard about?

c What can ordinary people do to 'reduce their carbon footprint' in everyday life?

✕ **Extra:** Make a list of the things that you do personally to reduce your carbon footprint – coming to school by bike, for example.

Future Dreaming (A short story)

You are going to read the short story *Future Dreaming* by the Australian writer George Ivanoff.

A Reading for gist

Written texts
▶ 3.1

1. Read through the whole story once. Don't check the meaning of every word. Rather, concentrate on getting a general understanding of who the people in the story are and what happens (the 'storyline' or 'plot').
2. Work in groups with 'Placemats' to compare what you understood, then share your ideas in class.

The storm raged. The water rose, flooding fields, gardens and buildings. The wind howled with tremendous force, sweeping away all that stood in its path. Rain fell from the dark sky in torrential bursts.

Standing in the middle of this violence was a boy. The wind whipped his wet sandy-coloured hair about his sad face. As he stared pitifully at all the devastation, he silently mouthed a single word: "Help!"

Jade was wet. Her eyes snapped open. She was huddled under her doona, soaked with sweat. It was a cold, crisp morning, but she felt unbearably hot. Kicking off the doona, she closed her eyes again. Images from her dream drifted behind her eyelids. She tried to remember the details of the boy's face. But all she could see was the sadness in his eyes and the single word on his lips.

Jade opened her eyes, suddenly realising that she was cold. She pulled the doona back over herself and shivered. Then she looked over at the clock on the bedside table and yelped. The alarm hadn't gone off. And she was going to be late for school if she didn't get a move on. She threw the doona off again, wrapped her dressing gown around her pyjamas and rushed out of her room to get some breakfast.

"Bit late this morning," said her mother, looking up from her cup of coffee and her copy of the *Financial Review*.

"Forgot to set the alarm," explained Jade as she opened the refrigerator and stuck her head in.

1 *rage:* happen in a violent way
2 *howl:* blow strongly
2 *sweep sth. away:* destroy sth. and carry it off
3 *torrential burst:* kurzer sintflutartiger Regenguss
4 *whip sth.:* etwas peitschen
5 *pitifully:* sadly
5 *devastation:* Verwüstung
7 *snap open:* open suddenly
7 *huddled:* (here) zusammengerollt
7 *doona (Australian English):* Bettdecke
8 *soaked:* durchnässt
8 *sweat:* Schweiß
8 *unbearably:* unerträglich
10 *eyelid:* Augenlid
13 *shiver:* zittern
14 *yelp:* give a short, loud shout
19 *set the alarm:* den Wecker stellen

Her mother nodded and sipped at her coffee. "Sleep well?"

Jade emerged with a carton of orange juice. "Um ... not really." She took a swig from the carton.

"Would you please use a glass?" said Jade's mother, shaking her head.

Jade took another swig. "I will next time." Then she put the carton back.

"You were calling out in your sleep again last night," said Karen, Jade's older sister.

"You having dreams again?" asked their mother.

"Uh-huh," nodded Jade, getting a slice of bread from the freezer and heading for the toaster.

"Well, could you try for quieter dreams tonight," said Karen, yawning and reaching for the jar of instant coffee. "I've got a paper due tomorrow."

"Maybe you should see someone about those nightmares," said their mother, putting down her newspaper.

Jade shifted uncomfortably as she waited for her toast.

"Want a lift to school?" asked Karen, trying the change of subject. "I'm leaving in ten, and I could drive past your school on the way to uni."

"Cool," said Jade, grabbing her toast as it popped up. "I'd better get dressed." She took a huge bite from the piece of dry toast and chucked the rest into the compost container, then headed for her room.

Karen got stuck in the morning peak traffic and Jade was late for school after all. She got a warning from her homeroom teacher and sniggers from her classmates as she tried to sneak into the classroom. As she slumped into her chair, she thought that she would have been better off catching the train.

"And finally this morning," said their teacher, "I'd like to welcome Marc Rider to our school. He and his parents have just moved into the area." The teacher smiled. "Stand up Marc, so the others can see who you are."

A blond-haired boy near the front of the class got tentatively to his feet. He looked around at the staring faces, smiled nervously and quickly sat down again.

"I trust you will all make Marc feel very welcome," said the teacher. "Now, off to your first class."

As kids started jostling for the door, Jade stared at the new boy – the new boy who looked very familiar.

* * *

Jade watched the new boy for the rest of the day. She watched him from a distance as he ran around the oval at recess, unsuccessfully trying to join in with the other boys. She stared at the back of his head throughout the day's classes. At lunchtime she sat on one of the benches in the quadrangle, not too far from where he was sitting. She watched him as he ate his sandwich and drank his can of cola. As she watched him, she finally realised that he reminded her of the boy from her dream.

Marc couldn't be the boy from her dream, Jade decided as she ate her own sandwich. It was impossible! Besides, Marc's hair was a little darker, his nose was not quite the same, and he was definitely younger. Still ... he did look an awful lot like the boy in her dream. Much too similar to be a coincidence.

Having finished her sandwich, Jade got the apple out of her lunch box. As she bit into it, she looked up to see Marc bite into his apple and look up.

21 *sip:* drink a small mouthful
22 *swig:* large mouthful
32 *instant coffee:* Pulverkaffee, löslicher Kaffee
32 *paper:* (here) Referat
33 *nightmare:* Alptraum
37 *in ten:* in 10 minutes
38 *grab sth.:* take sth. in your hand quickly
39 *chuck sth.:* throw sth.
39 *compost container:* Kompostbehälter
41 *peak traffic:* Hauptverkehrszeit
41 *homeroom teacher:* Klassenlehrer/in
42 *snigger:* Kichern
43 *slump:* plumpsen
48 *tentatively:* nervously
52 *jostle:* drängeln
53 *familiar:* bekannt
55 *oval:* Laufbahn
55 *recess:* (school) break
57 *bench:* Sitzbank
57 *quadrangle:* Schulhof, Innenhof
64 *coincidence:* (reiner) Zufall

Their eyes met. He smiled and she immediately looked away. When she looked up again, he was walking off, shoulders slumped. As he passed a rubbish bin, he chucked out his empty drink can and the remainder of his apple. Jade watched thoughtfully as he walked away.

When she finished her apple, Jade put the core back into her lunch box. She would take it home and put it into the compost. It was only then that it occurred to Jade that Marc had been eating alone. She wondered where he was from, who his parents were and why he reminded her of the boy in her dream.

"You're a bit weird, aren't you?"

Jade whirled round. Lunchtime was nearly over, but she was still sitting on the bench, alone, lost in thought. Marc must have snuck up behind her.

"Am not!" was all Jade could think of saying in return.

"You've been looking at me strangely all day," said Marc, walking around to the front of the bench. "And now you're just sitting here on your own, staring at nothing. I think that's a bit weird."

"Oh ..." replied Jade, realising she couldn't really argue the point. "Sorry!" It's just that you ... kinda remind me of someone."

"Someone nice, I hope," said Marc, sitting on the bench next to her.

"Don't know," said Jade, looking down at her lunch box, remembering the dream.

"What do you mean you don't know?" asked Marc, puzzled.

"Well ... I don't really know the person you remind me of." She didn't look up as she said this. She realised that what she was saying probably did make her sound rather odd.

"See," said Marc, smirking. "Weird!"

Jade looked up and glared at him. Maybe she was being a bit weird, but she didn't need some misfit new kid telling her so. "Well at least I don't throw cans into the rubbish bin when there's a recycling bin right next to it," she blurted out.

They stared at each other for a few seconds, neither of them knowing what to say next, when the bell, signalling the end of lunchtime, rang. Then suddenly, embarrassed by her outburst, Jade grabbed her lunch box and rushed off without another word.

Marc watched her go and shook his head slowly.

"Weird!"

* * *

"Help!"

The sandy-haired boy was alone and he was nowhere. There was nothing around him. There was nothing ... anywhere. His hair was matted with sweat. His face was red and damp. His eyes were sad and empty. His lips, cracked and dry. His eyelids started to flutter uncontrollably, and his eyes rolled back, till there was only white. He crumpled, like a puppet whose strings had been cut. Jade struggled to get to the boy.

70 *slumped:* rounded, leaning forward
72 *remainder:* rest
75 *core:* Kerngehäuse
77 *occur to sb.:* jdm etwas einfallen
81 *weird:* strange, unusual
82 *whirl round:* turn quickly
83 *sneak up (past tense = snuck):* sich anschleichen
89 *kinda (= kind of):* irgendwie
96 *odd:* seltsam
97 *smirk:* smile in a way that says 'I'm right'
98 *glare at sb.:* stare at sb. angrily
99 *misfit:* Außenseiter-
100 *blurt out:* herausplatzen
103 *outburst:* angry words
109 *matted:* stuck together
110 *cracked:* rissig
110 *flutter:* flattern
112 *crumple:* fall down lifeless
112 *puppet:* Marionette
112 *struggle:* fight

Something was holding her back, stopping her legs from running, her arms from working.

A voice from the darkness called: "Jade, are you OK?"

She opened her eyes. Her mother's concerned face looked down at her.

"What?" asked Jade, confused.

"You've had another nightmare," whispered her mother.

"Oh." She propped herself up on an elbow. "Sorry!"

"How about I make you some hot chocolate?" asked her mother, not really knowing what else to do.

Jade nodded with a half-smile. Hot chocolate! It was her mother's solution to everything from skinned knees to family crisis, from the death of a pet to ... bad dreams. It meant she had something to do and didn't have to talk about it.

As she got up to follow her mother to the kitchen, Jade shivered, despite being drenched in sweat.

* * *

Jade waited outside the school counsellor's office, hoping that no one would see her there. Her mother had driven her to school early and was talking with the counsellor – talking about her; talking about her dreams.

The door finally opened and her mother came out.

"You've got an appointment to see Ms Helmond at lunchtime today."

"Mum, I don't ..." began Jade.

"I'd really feel happier if you talked to someone about your dreams," said her mother, cutting her off. "Please!"

Jade looked down at her shoes, sighed, and then nodded. Her mother wasn't a good talker, or listener for that matter, so Jade wasn't really surprised that she was getting her daughter to talk through her problems with a complete stranger.

"Thank you," said her mother. "Now I've got to get to work."

She gave her daughter a quick hug and rushed off. As Jade watched her mother leaving, she noticed Marc walking past. He had a drink can in his hand and a school bag over one shoulder. He stopped by the bins and looked over at her. Then, smiling, he made a big show of dropping the can into the recycle bin rather than the rubbish bin, before continuing on his way.

* * *

"And you're having these dreams every night?" asked Ms Helmond, the school counsellor, as she shuffled through the papers in Jade's file.

"Pretty much," answered Jade.

Ms Helmond nodded as she continued to look through the file.

"Hmmm," murmured Ms Helmond, head down. "You took part in the school's recycling drive last year." She continued to shuffle

119 *prop yourself up:* sich aufstützen
123 *skinned:* abgeschürft
127 *school counsellor:* Beratungslehrer/in, Schulpsychologe/in
131 *appointment:* Termin
134 *cut sb. off:* interrupt sb.
136 *for that matter:* was das betrifft
139 *hug:* Umarmung
141 *bin:* Abfalleimer
146 *shuffle through sth.:* etwas durchblättern
147 *file:* Akte
148 *pretty much:* more or less
153 *drive:* Aktion

through papers. "You wrote a piece for the school magazine on climate change."

Jade nodded as Ms Helmond looked up.

"Environmental issues are really important to you, aren't they Jade?"

Jade nodded again.

"Would you say that climate change and damage to our environment is something that worries you?"

"I guess," answered Jade. "I mean ... I do think about it a bit. You know ... pollution and recycling and stuff."

Ms Helmond nodded thoughtfully. She closed Jade's file and folded her hands together on top of it before looking up at her.

"I think your dreams may simply be manifestations of your anxieties. It's your subconscious telling you that you need to do something to help the world. That's why the boy is asking for help. Maybe, deep down, you're even feeling a little guilty because you're not doing everything that you can."

She smiled. It was a self-satisfied sort of smile that said *I've figured it out, aren't I wonderful.*

"I think you'll find," she continued, "that if you start doing something proactive – saving water, recycling, or whatever – that your subconscious will settle down and the dreams will stop."

She picked up Jade's file, indicating that the session was at an end.

Jade nodded and reached for her school bag.

"So are you nuts?" asked Marc as Jade stepped out of the counsellor's office.

"What are you doing here!" asked Jade, surprised to see him waiting there for her.

"I got lonely eating my lunch with no one staring at me," he smiled, holding up his lunch box.

"Yeah ... funny," said Jade, scowling at him.

"So ... are you?"

"Huh?"

"Are you nuts?"

"No!" said Jade indignantly. "I'm not nuts."

"Then why were you seeing the counsellor?" persisted Marc. "Is it because you keep staring at new kids in a weird kinda way?"

"None of your business," said Jade stalking off. "Get lost!"

"I was just joking," said Marc, following after her. "I don't really think you're nuts."

Jade continued walking.

"Wanna have lunch together?" he said. "I haven't eaten mine yet."

Jade walked over to the quadrangle, dumped her bag on a bench and slumped down beside it. Marc sat down on the other side of the bag. They both brought out their lunches in silence. Neither of them said anything while they ate. After they were finished, Marc threw his can into the recycle, and then went to put his apple core in the bin.

"I'll take that," said Jade, snatching the core from his hand.

He looked at her strangely.

"Um ..." Marc shrugged.

"Great!" said Jade. "I thought that you might ... I dunno ... have some idea ... something to say ... maybe ..." Her voiced trailed off and she looked away.

166 *I guess:* yes, probably
170 *manifestation:* Erscheinungsform
170 *anxiety:* worry
171 *subconscious:* Unterbewusstsein
174 *self-satisfied:* selbstgefällig
174 *figure sth. out:* find an answer to sth.
176 *do sth. proactive:* die Initiative ergreifen
179 *indicate sth.:* etwas anzeigen
180 *nod:* (mit dem Kopf) nicken
181 *nuts:* crazy
186 *scowl at sb.:* look angrily at sb.
190 *indignant:* empört
191 *persist:* nicht locker lassen
193 *none of your business:* das geht dich nichts an
193 *get lost:* hau ab
197 *wanna* = do you want to
198 *dump sth.:* put sth. down, drop sth.
201 *can:* Dose
203 *snatch sth. from sb.:* jdm. etwas entreißen
205 *shrug:* mit den Schultern zucken
206 *dunno* = I don't know
207 *trail off:* become quieter and quieter

"Compost," she said, explaining her actions. "We have a compost bin at home."

"Oh." nodded Marc.

"Yeah, I know, that probably makes me even weirder," said Jade.

Then the bell rang and they headed off for class.

* * *

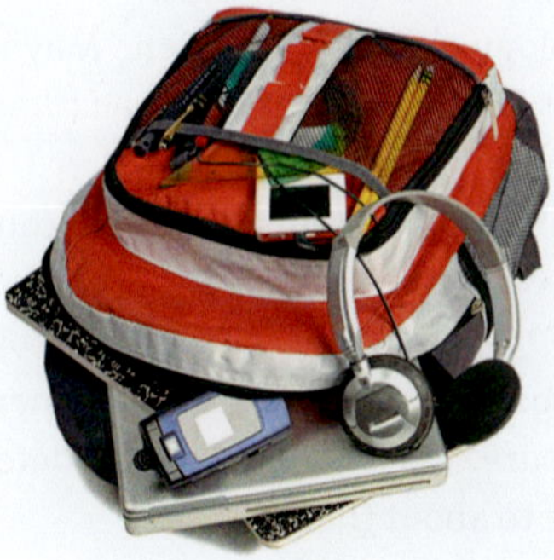

"So how did it go?" asked Karen, as Jade walked into the kitchen.

Jade shrugged as she dumped her school bag on the floor by the table. She headed to the refrigerator and got the carton of orange juice.

"Glass," reminded Karen, before Jade had the chance to put the carton to her lips.

Jade nodded and got herself a glass before sitting down at the table, opposite her sister. She filled it up with juice, drained the glass and refilled it.

"Come on," coaxed Karen. "Spill the beans. What did the counsellor say?"

Jade sighed. "She reckons I'm worried about the environment and that I just need to do something positive to make the dreams go away."

"What?"

"She said that my dreams were just *manifestations of my anxieties.*"

Jade sipped at her juice.

"But that doesn't make sense," complained Karen. "You've been having these dreams, on and off, since you were a little kid. I doubt that you were all that worried about the environment when you were five."

Jade shrugged and drank some more juice.

"What kind of counsellor is she?" railed Karen. "I mean ..."

Karen's voice trailed off as realisation dawned on her. She stared intently at her younger sister. "You didn't tell her the whole story, did you?"

Jade shrugged and stared into her glass of juice.

"Well, what did you tell her?"

"Not much, really," admitted Jade, looking up. "Mum talked to her this morning and told her about my dreams. And I guess she didn't tell her that I used to have them when I was little."

Karen stared at her sister.

"So I guess it's Mum's fault," said Jade, looking down at her juice again. She suddenly felt guilty about blaming her mother.

"To be fair," said Karen, "Mum probably doesn't even remember you had bad dreams when you were little. She was working an awful lot back then, and I was the one taking care of you."

Karen shook her head and turned to stare out the window. She ran a hand through her short blond hair and sighed. "OK," she started. "I think there's something I should tell you."

Jade looked up.

"I've had the dreams too," Karen announced. "Not for a long time now. But when I was younger, I had them for a little while. The dreams were always about bad weather – storms and things. And there was someone in them. A kid. I could never really tell if it was a boy or a girl." She looked back at Jade. "They didn't last

221 *drain sth.:* drink until sth. is empty
222 *coax sb.:* jdn. langsam überreden
222 *spill the beans:* Erzähl schon.
223 *sigh:* seufzen
223 *reckon:* (here) be of the opinion
229 *on and off:* immer mal wieder
232 *rail:* schimpfen
232 *I mean:* (here) mal ehrlich
233 *realisation dawned on her:* es dämmmerte ihr/ es wurde ihr klar
233 *intently:* closely and carefully
237 *admit sth.:* etwas zugeben
242 *feel guilty:* ein schlechtes Gewissen haben
242 *blame sb.:* jdm. die Schuld für etwas geben
244 *an awful lot:* eine ganze Menge

all that long. I had a few when I was about ten. And then again a couple of years later."

"Wow!" exclaimed Jade.

"Yeah," agreed Karen.

"So ... they're probably not ordinary bad dreams, then?" said Jade.

"Probably," agreed Karen.

"So what are they?" asked Jade. "And what do they mean?"

"I've got a friend studying psychology, " suggested Karen. "Maybe we ..."

"No," Jade interrupted. "No thanks."

"What about ..." started Karen.

"I'm OK, really," Jade cut in. "I never wanted to see the counsellor in the first place."

"But ..."

"Look," said Jade, interrupting again. "I've always known there's something more to these dreams. And now I'm sure." She suddenly looked determined. "And I think I know who I should be talking to about them."

* * *

Jade dreamt of the storm again that night ... and the boy. The storm was not as severe. The boy did not look as sad.

"To save the future, start with the present," said the boy. His voice was familiar. "Each step is important, and each individual can make a difference."

* * *

Marc came and sat next to Jade at lunch the next day.

"Sorry about being grumpy yesterday," said Jade, as she began eating her lunch. "I haven't been sleeping well."

After they had finished their apples, Marc automatically placed his core in Jade's lunch box. Jade looked up at him and he smiled.

"I've been having weird dreams," started Jade.

She told him all about the dreams, about the session with the school counsellor, and about her talk with her sister. Then they sat in silence for a few minutes, until Jade looked towards Marc expectantly.

"Wow!" exclaimed Marc, eyes wide.

"Is that all you've got to say?" asked Jade.

"What?" said Marc. "Have a neat solution for you? Be able to explain everything?" He shrugged again, wracking his brains for something more to say – something to make Jade feel better about having told him everything. "Maybe ... maybe the dreams are messages."

Jade turned slowly to look at him. "Messages?"

"Yeah. Messages from ... aliens or something."

Jade began to turn away again.

"No! Not aliens. Maybe ... the dreams are messages from the future?"

Jade looked interested.

"Maybe things have gotten so bad with the environment," he continued, "that these future-people are desperate to get people in the past – that'd be us – to change their ways ... to start caring more for the environment ... and ... change the

268 *determined:* entschlossen
271 *severe:* strong, bad
275 *grumpy:* in a bad mood
282 *expectantly:* erwartungsvoll
285 *a neat solution:* eine saubere/klare Lösung
286 *wrack one's brains:* sich den Kopf zerbrechen
295 *desperate:* wanting very much to do sth.

future ... make it better..."

"And they're doing this with dreams?" Jade raised an eyebrow.

"Well, maybe that's the only way of getting messages to the past." Marc was on a roll now. "First they tried your sister, but she didn't listen. And now they're trying you." he grinned at her. "You could be the chosen one. The one destined to save the world."

Jade looked back sceptically.

Suddenly they both burst into laughter.

"Dreams ... from the future," laughed Jade.

"To change the world," laughed Marc.

"As if!" they both hollered together.

As their laughter petered out, they both looked around at the school grounds they were in.

On the next bench, they saw someone eating a banana. A teacher walked along the path eating an apple. A young kid dropped a half-eaten sandwich into a bin.

"It's a pity the school doesn't have a compost bin," sighed Jade.

"Well," said Marc. "There's no reason why it shouldn't."

"Yeah," agreed Jade, thoughts of starting a school compost heap running through her mind. "You're absolutely right."

* * *

There were no storms in Jade's dreams that night. The sun was shining and a pleasantly cool breeze blew across the water. The boy was standing on the golden sand as the water gently lapped at his feet. He was smiling.

"Thank you," he said. "The future isn't certain. So many things can happen. But you've given it a chance."

His familiar eyes sparkled.

"Thanks ... Great-Gran."

Jade woke up smiling ... and wondering.

[From: *Under the Weather, Stories About Climate Change,* 2009]

298 *raise an eyebrow:* eine Augenbraue hochziehen
299 *be on a roll:* in Fahrt kommen
301 *grin:* smile in a friendly way
301 *the chosen one:* die Auserwählte
301 *destined:* bestimmt
307 *holler:* shout
308 *school grounds:* Schulgelände
308 *peter out:* come slowly to an end
317 *breeze:* light wind
318 *lap:* plätschern
321 *sparkle:* funkeln
322 *Great-Gran* = great-grandmother (Urgroßmutter)

B Understanding the story

Working in groups and on projects
▶ 1

1. A good way to understand a story is to use diagrams. Form groups to look at the following aspects of the story in more depth. Your group should look at one aspect and report to the class using your finished diagram.

   a **Jade, her mother and her sister**

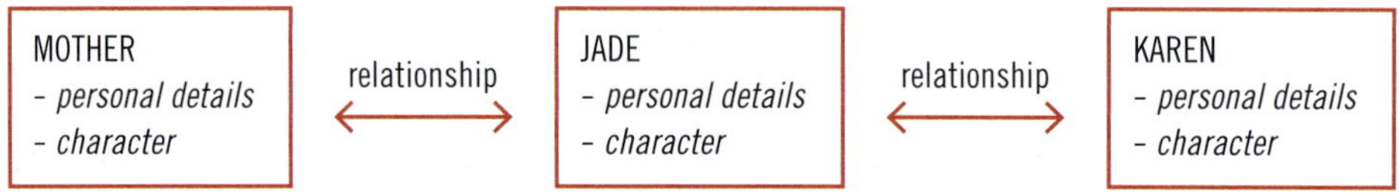

   b **Jade and Marc**
   Describe the key moments in the relationship between Jade and Marc (when Jade first sees him, their first meeting etc.), and then outline how their relationship develops during the story.

   c **Jade's dreams**
   What are the different dreams Jade has and how do they develop during the story? What happens in Jade's life to change the dreams?

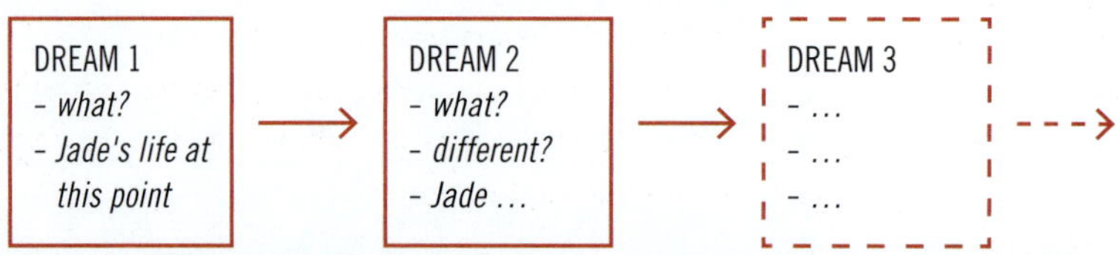

Activity chest
▶ 9

2. Now look together in class at the main theme which runs right through the story: the explanation of Jade's dreams. Talk about the following questions, then divide into groups to draw your own diagram to illustrate your ideas. Show your diagram to the class with a 'Gallery walk'.
   a What effect do the dreams at the beginning of the story have on Jade? Why?
   b Why is the arrival of Marc at the school important for understanding her dreams?
   c What explanations of the dreams are given by the adults in the story?
   d Why is the conversation in the kitchen with Karen significant?
   e How does Marc explain Jade's dreams?
   f What does Jade's last dream suggest about whether Marc is right or wrong?

C Analysing the story

Written texts
▶ 2.3a

You are now going to look at how the story is told, why the writer has chosen certain formats and devices, and how a reader could react to these. Work through all the tasks below in groups, then at the end share your ideas in class.

1. State in your own words the 'message' of this story. (Take the title into account in your answer).
2. Explain how the writer uses the story to get this message across. Consider the following aspects:
   - The use of a teenage central protagonist. (Who does the reader identify with in the story? Why? How do the young people compare with the adults in the story?)
   - A story structure that keeps the reader interested and wanting to know what happens next (suspense). How is this done? What is the effect of the 'ending' on the reader?
   - How the central topic of the story (global warming) is presented through dreams. (Nature of the dreams? The reader's likely reaction to the boy in the dream?)
   - The use of the 'symbol' of the compost bin. (Symbol of what? What part does it play in the relationship between Jade and Marc?)
3. Analyse the writing techniques used by the author and their effect on the reader. Take the following points into account:
   - The narrative perspective. (Who tells the story? What is the effect of this narrative perspective on the reader?)
   - Does the story 'tell and explain' or 'show directly'? (How much of the story is told through dialogues? What do we learn in the dialogues about the characters' thoughts / feelings / relationships with one another? How do the dreams make an abstract idea concrete?)
   - What rhetorical devices does the writer use, why, and with what effect? (Images? Choice of words: dramatic, emotional, ...? Language and rhetorical devices used in the dream sequences?)

Written texts
▶ 4.2

D Reacting to the story

Written texts
▶ 5.2e

There are several ways in which you could react to the story. Work in groups to choose one of the following, then present your results to the class.

a Re-tell the story from the point of view of another character.

Written texts
▶ 2.3b

b Choose an important scene from the story and act it out using the original dialogue – the first conversation between Jade and Marc, for example.

c Re-tell the story as a science-fiction story set in the future. Imagine how it is arranged for the boy in the dream to contact his ancestors.

Sound and (moving) images
▶ 3

d Imagine you wanted to make a film of the story. Choose one of the scenes and develop a 'storyboard'. Which famous actors would you choose to play the roles?

Written texts
▶ 5.2d

e Write a review of the story for a school magazine.

REFERENCE SECTION

Activity chest

Appointments Calendar

Time	Partner
10.00 h	
12.00 h	
14.00 h	

▶ 1 Appointments

Purpose: finding a partner to work with
- Make an appointments calendar and fill in a partner's name for each time.
- Keep the calendar in your file so you can use it each time for this activity.
- The teacher gives you a task and the time to use: for example, 12 o'clock. Your regular partner for 12 o'clock is the student you work with for the task.

▶ 2 Brainstorming

Purpose: collecting ideas
- You can do this alone, but more usually in a group.
- Use a large sheet of paper.
- Write down (in a group you can have a 'secretary' for this) *any* ideas that come into your mind. At this stage, it is not important to think how 'good' or 'bad' they are. Be creative!
- Then look through and cross out ideas that are not relevant or helpful.
- Agree on and list your final ideas. It often helps to put the 'best' ideas at the top of your list.

▶ 3 Bus stop

Purpose: finding a partner to work with
- Decide on two or three places in the classroom which are 'bus stops'.
- Work alone on your task. When you have finished, go to one of the bus stops.
- Your partner is a student who is already at, or comes to your bus stop.

▶ 4 Cheat sheets (Spickzettel)

Purpose: summarising a text for a short talk
- Go through the text underlining or noting down key words and phrases.
- List the words and phrases on a small piece of paper. Cross out *all* words that are not absolutely necessary. Ideally, you should have only one key word for each part of the text.
- Use the 'cheat sheet' to give your summary. Use the key words to remind yourself of what you need to say, but otherwise use your own words as far as possible. Do not simply repeat the original text.

► 5 Double circles

Purpose: comparing your ideas with those of other students

- Arrange your classroom so that students can sit opposite each other in pairs: put chairs in 'double circles' in the centre of the room, or on both sides of rows of tables in a horseshoe.
- Begin the activity. Work with the student opposite you. Then when your teacher tells you to, students on the outside move clockwise around the circle / horseshoe. Continue until you have spoken to 3-6 other students.

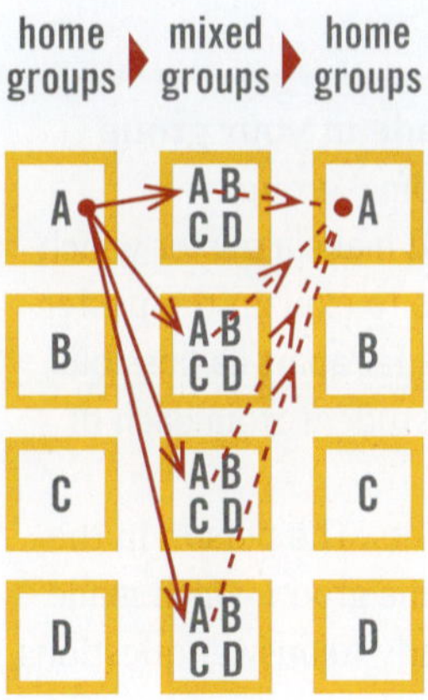

► 6 Expert groups

Purpose: studying several texts (or a longer text in sections)

- Divide the class into groups of 3-4. Give each group a letter name (A, B, C, ...), one letter for each of the texts / sections you are going to study. For four texts, you will need groups named A, B, C, D. These A, B, C, D groups are called your 'home groups'.
- In your home group, study 'your' text: you have to become 'the experts' on it and prepare a short talk so that you can explain it to others who do not know it.
- Form new groups. Each new group should have in it students from an A group, a B group, a C group and a D group. Give your talk to your mixed group. The others in the group listen, take notes, and if necessary ask you questions.
- Return to your home group and, in turns, report back what you learned about the other texts, comparing your ideas and correcting any points if necessary. Produce a summary together of all the texts / sections.

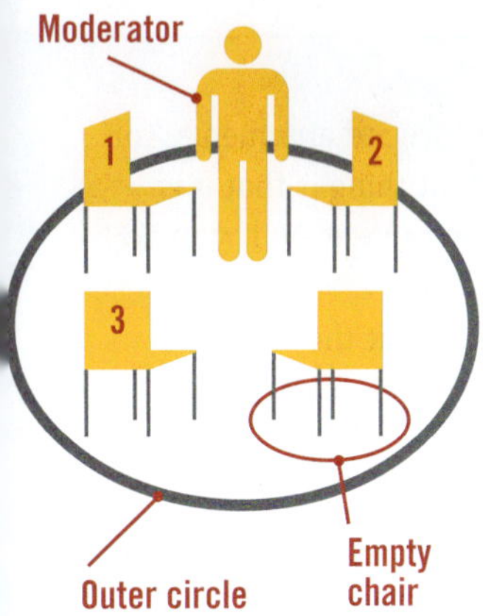

► 7 Fish-bowl

Purpose: discussing a topic as a class

- Work in groups to collect and make notes of your ideas for the task you have been given.
- When you have done this, you are ready to begin the discussion. The teacher can lead the discussion (be the 'moderator') or you can choose a student.
- Choose a person from your group to sit on one of the chairs in the middle of your classroom – in the 'fish-bowl'. In the diagram there are three chairs, but you can have more (or choose more than one person from your group to sit in the fish-bowl).
- All the other students now sit round the fish-bowl in the outer circle.
- Your group representatives put forward your group's ideas, but any student can at any time join the discussion by going into the fish-bowl and sitting on the empty chair. This can be to add a point to what your representative has said – or to disagree if necessary.
- At the end of the discussion everyone goes to sit in the outer circle. Now you can talk as a whole class about what you have heard.

► 8 Freeze-frames (freeze-frame tableaux)

Purpose: 'bringing alive' a situation, theme, etc. that you have read about

- Your teacher gives you a theme for your tableau, or asks you to choose one (e.g. from a story or poem) to illustrate with a tableau.
- Work in groups. Your task is to show the situation or theme by standing, sitting, etc. as a group in a such a way that people looking can see and understand what is

happening and the ideas, feelings and so on behind the situation. You can only stand, sit, etc. – you must not move!
- It often helps to choose one person in your group to be a 'director' – to help everyone build the tableau.
- In groups, one at a time, show your tableau to the class. Allow plenty of time for the other students to look at it and discuss it.
- You can also add to your tableau the idea of a 'reporter'. This can be a student from your group who can use an (imagined) microphone to interview one of the characters in the tableau, or students from the class can come and interview a character.
- Explain your tableau to the class, then the class should comment on it.

▶ 9 Gallery walk

Purpose: presenting and explaining to the class a poster made in your group
- Divide the class into groups of 4-5 students. These are your 'home' groups.
- In your home group, work on the task you have been given and make a poster which shows your ideas, etc. Every person in your group must be able to explain the poster.
- Put up the posters of all the groups on the classroom walls – as far apart as possible.
- Make new groups of 4-5. Each new group must have in it one student from each of the old (home) groups.
- When the teacher tells you, each group goes to one of the posters. The person in the group who is the expert on the poster (the person from the home group which made it), explains the poster to the others. Experts should also be ready to answer questions.
- Move round in your groups until you have seen all the posters.
- Discuss in class all the posters you saw – which did you like best? why?

▶ 10 Panel discussions

Purpose: to discuss the pros and cons of an argument
- Divide the class first into two halves. One half is going to put forward arguments 'for' something, the other half the arguments 'against'. The important thing is that it is your task to argue your case in front of the class as well as you can – even if you do not necessarily agree with it. Be convincing!
- Each half talks about their topic and finds 3-4 important points that they want to make. One student can be the 'secretary' and list these on a large piece of paper.
- Then each half divides into smaller groups – one group for each of the key aspects – and works to develop ideas about it. After a given time, choose a group speaker.
- Put chairs at the front of the classroom for the speakers. They can sit in a row facing the class, or the 'for' and 'against' speakers can sit opposite each other in two groups.
- The discussion now proceeds as follows. A speaker from a 'for' group presents his / her ideas (no longer than two minutes). Then a speaker from an 'against' group presents his / her ideas (two minutes again). Now these two speakers have one minute to react to what each has just said – so if the 'for' speaker hears an 'against' argument that he / she wants to reply to immediately, this can be done in the minute. Continue like this until all group speakers have spoken and reacted.
- Now, in your original groups again, collect and list all the points you heard in the discussion both 'for' and 'against'. Who do you think won the discussion and why? Each group in turn tells the class its final opinion (with the reasons). You can also organise a vote.

▶ 11 Peer review (Peer conferences)

Purpose: correcting and improving a text you have written

- The teacher gives you a writing task. When everyone in the class has a finished text, form groups of 3-4.
- In the groups, pass round everyone's text, so that you all read all the texts. When you read, your aim is to look for language mistakes, how well the text is structured (its 'logic'), how clear the ideas are, etc., so that the writer can afterwards correct and improve the text.
- You can write your comments directly on to the text, or as a group you can develop a 'checklist', like the one below.
- Discuss your comments with the writer of the text. For example, ask what something means if it is not clear, and point out errors.
- Be sure to give positive as well as negative feedback! Say what you think is good as well as what is bad.

	TEXT 1	TEXT 2	TEXT 3
Language mistakes?			
Good title?			
Logical and clear?			
...?			

▶ 12 Placemats

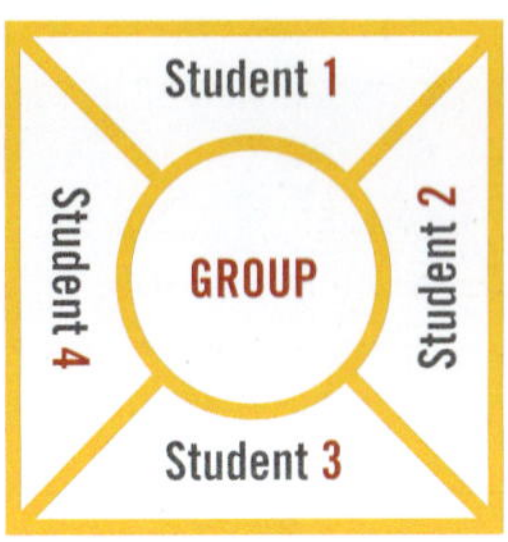

Purpose: collecting ideas in a group

- Work in groups of 3-4 (the diagram shows four students).
- Place a large sheet of paper in the middle of your group table. Mark out the paper as shown in the diagram with sections around the outside for students and a circle (or square) in the centre for the group as a whole.
- Each student begins by writing his / her own ideas in their place on the placemat.
- After a given time, look at what everyone has written, and by discussing together, agree on those ideas which represent what everyone in the group thinks.
- Write these into the centre of the placemat. You can now use the group's ideas to make a group report.

▶ 13 Think-Pair-Share (T-P-S)

Purpose: comparing your ideas with a partner's

- Think about your task and make notes – it may be a list of ideas, key words, etc. Your teacher may give you a time limit for this.
- Find a partner. First one student, then the second, presents his / her ideas to the other. Don't show your ideas to your partner, say them out loud. When you listen to your partner, be ready to interrupt with questions and comments.
- You can now tell the class your ideas: one student can speak for both of you, or you can report separately.

▶ 14 Silent discussions

Purpose: discussing a topic in a group – but in writing, not with spoken words

- Place a large sheet of paper on the table in the middle of your group. In the centre, write the topic, theme, question, etc. that you are going to discuss.
- Write your ideas onto the sheet. It is easier to understand if each student writes in a different place on the sheet and uses a different colour.
- When everyone has written their first ideas, begin to read what others have written on the sheet and add your comments to them – just as you would reply in a conversation.
- When all the group has finished writing, you can look through all the ideas and begin to organise / summarise them.

▶ 15 Walk-Talk-Write

Purpose: collecting ideas as a class

- Put up large sheets of paper around the classroom (as far apart as possible). On each sheet there is a question or topic you have to think about – an 'impulse'.
- Divide into groups. There should be as many groups as there are pieces of paper.
- In your groups, collect ideas about all the impulses.
- When your teacher tells you, each group goes to one of the pieces of paper and writes up its ideas.
- Now, in groups, move round clockwise to the next piece of paper. Read and discuss the ideas that are written on it and add your own. You can go round all the pieces of paper more than once, adding new ideas and comments each time.
- At the end, talk as a class about the ideas that were collected.

Written texts

▶ 1 Working with written texts in your exams

In class tests and exams, you can generally speaking expect three basic tasks on a written text:

Understanding the text (comprehension): showing you understand **what** is said.
Analysing the text (analysis): showing you understand **why** and **how** a text is written in a particular way.
Reacting to the text: showing you can **express an opinion** about the text, or use it as a basis for **creative writing** (an email, story, newspaper article, etc. that you write yourself).

▶ 2 Non-fictional and fictional texts

Texts can be divided into two kinds:

Non-fictional texts deal with real people, events, etc. in the real world. They include newspaper articles, emails and letters, reports, blogs, brochures and advertisements.
Fictional texts deal with people, events, etc. that are **imagined by a writer**. They include stories, plays, poems and songs.

▶ 2.1 Non-fictional text types

Non-fictional texts can be divided into different **text types.** These **categories** depend on the main **aim of the text.**

Category 1: Informative	These give **information**: their aim is to **inform** the reader. Informative texts are sometimes further divided into three groups: - **purely factual** (just facts: a railway timetable, for example), - **descriptive** (describe a person, place, event, etc.), - **expository** (give facts, but also **explain them** and often **add comments and opinions**).
Category 2: Argumentative	These **express an opinion** by **discussing** a topic with the reader – usually showing the **arguments** 'for' and 'against' something.
Category 3: Persuasive	These try to **persuade** or **influence** the reader. A typical example is an advertisement.
Category 4: Instructive	These tell the reader **how to do something.** An example is the **instructions** which come with a new mobile phone. (This is probably the type you meet least in your exam.)

NOTE: Most texts do not belong in just one category. A 'persuasive' advertisement, can also 'inform' the reader; an 'argumentative' text also tries to 'persuade' the reader that a particular opinion is the right one. It is, therefore, better in most cases to talk of a **dominant text type:** the most important basic category.

▶ 2.2 Examples of non-fictional text types

a **Advertisement (ad or advert)**

Dominant text type: **persuasive**.

Important features:

- **how** the advertisement tries to **influence** the reader through text (**advertising blurb**), **pictures** and **design** (colours, size of the text);
- advertisements in Europe and many other parts of the world are **strictly controlled**: they must be 'legal, decent, honest and truthful'. However, advertisers sometimes use **hidden ways** to influence consumers. One example is 'greenwashing'.

b Blog (weblog)

Dominant text type: all **categories**.

Important features:

- whatever the text type, most blogs are **personal** – written by one person or a particular group of people about their personal experiences;
- blogs are an **electronic (online) medium** and typically use **links** to organise information. They can also be **multi-media**, with sound, video and pictures as well as text.

c Case study

Dominant text type: **informative**.

Important features:

- the aim of a case study is to use a **specific example** of something to make clear a **general situation.** An example would be one person's individual story about a problem they have had online to help readers to understand the general problems that everyone can have when they use the internet;
- when you read a case study look for (a) the specific details of what it tells you, then (b) how these facts, etc. can relate to a bigger picture. How could other people find themselves in a similar situation? How could their experiences be the same or different? How typical is the example in the case study? What could readers learn from the case study? (Perhaps to have the same success as the person in the study, or to avoid the mistakes this person made.)

d Formal letter

Dominant text type: **argumentative**.

Important features:

- the example letter on page 27 **(a letter of application)** shows you the key features of a formal letter. The **layout** of the letter is fixed (addresses at the top, signature at the bottom, etc). The **beginning** *(Dear Ms Griggs)* **and ending** *(Yours sincerely)* are also fixed, and there is always a **subject line** *(Application for a work placement)*;
- formal letters have a particular **style**. The language is **formal** (polite) and many phrases are **standard** *(I would like to apply for … / As you will see from my enclosed CV / I look forward to hearing from you soon)*.

e Newspaper news article

Dominant text type: **informative** (expository).

Important features:

- the aim of a news article is to inform readers of things that have happened – events. Journalists often call these facts **hard news.** To help the reader understand the events, the journalist sometimes gives **background information** and adds **explanations** where necessary;
- to write the story, the journalist almost always interviews people involved in the events, and their words are given in the article as **quotes**;
- when we look through a newspaper as readers, we often choose the particular articles we want to read because they look interesting, and news stories always, therefore, begin with a **headline** which sums up the story. There is often also a photo which **catches our eye**. In addition, news stories also usually have a particular **structure**: they are clearly divided into **paragraphs** (often one sentence long), and the most **important paragraphs are put at the beginning of the**

story so that we read them first;

- good news stories (for example, in **quality newspapers**) give facts only. The journalist does not try to **influence** or **persuade** the reader about what to think. However, some articles (usually in **tabloid newspapers**) do contain a **hidden opinion** and do try to influence the reader. This kind of article is called **biased** (opposite: **unbiased / objective**).

f Newspaper leading article

Dominant text type: **argumentative**.

Important features:

- a leading article (also called a **leader**) is the place where the newspaper expresses its opinion about an event in the news, usually on a special page inside the paper. The key features are: the article has a **clear structure**, with the topic at the beginning, arguments for and against in the middle, and a conclusion; the language can sometimes be complex (good leaders are aimed at **educated readers**); the article may use the pronoun 'we' (= the newspaper), but more usually expresses opinions indirectly (for example, with the passive).

g Newspaper (or magazine) feature article

Dominant text type: **informative**.

Important features:

- feature articles are generally about topics of **general interest**. Often longer than news stories, they aim to both **inform** and **entertain** the reader at the same time with interesting facts about a topic;
- the structure of the article can vary, but it generally **introduces the topic** at the beginning, **gives information about it** in the middle, and **makes a comment** or draws a **conclusion** at the end.

h Report

Dominant text type: **informative**.

Important features:

- reports are generally written about a situation, event, etc. in order to give the reader **clear information.** This often happens in business, but there can also, for example, be a report by an au pair about his / her experiences;
- the essential aspect of a report is that the information must be **easy to understand**, so there is a standard **structure** (introduction, facts paragraph by paragraph, conclusion, name of the writer).

i Speech

Dominant text type: **persuasive**.

Important features:

- although a speech is **spoken**, you often have to look at it as a text;
- speeches are given by many people (by politicians, for example) in order to put across a very clear **opinion** and to **persuade** the **audience.** Speech makers, therefore, are careful to **address the audience** – talk directly to the people listening – and speak in a **highly personal way**;
- one of the key aspects of a speech is also the **language used**. It is often **dramatic** and **emotional,** and may contain a lot of **rhetorical devices** (▶ 4.2).

▶ 2.3 Fictional text types

Fictional texts are divided into:

Narrative texts	short stories, novels that **tell a story**
Drama	plays
Poems and songs	'lyrical' texts

NOTE: we do not normally classify fictional texts as 'informative', 'persuasive', etc.

a Narrative texts

Important features:

- **the narrator (the person who tells the story)**: the two most common narrators are (a) **someone in the story** (a **first person narrator** who uses the personal pronoun 'I'), and (b) a **third person narrator** who tells the reader about the events and who refers to the people in the story with the pronouns 'he' / 'she' / 'they'. This third person narrator is *not* the author, but simply someone outside the story who is an **observer** - someone who is watching the events. In most stories the third person narrator concentrates on the main character (the **protagonist**) and tells the story from his or her point of view.
- **the setting:** where and when the story takes place and the **atmosphere**;
- **the characters:** the people in the story. The main character is usually called the **protagonist;**
- **language:** the language of fictional texts is usually characterised by such things as **images** (▶ Rhetorical devices 4.2) and the **style** of the writer (the way an individual writer likes to use language);
- **structure:** stories are structured in particular ways to **get and hold the reader's attention**, and to tell the story so that it is **interesting to read**. One way the writer often does this is with **suspense –** introducing a **mystery** to which the reader wants to know the answer.

b Drama

Important features:

- plays are not written to be read but to be watched **on stage in a theatre.** This means that it is only possible to fully understand a play by also seeing **what is happening**;
- the essential element of all plays is the **characters**, the people in the play. Good plays show us a lot about their **feelings** and **emotions** in the situations in which they find themselves. Characters also usually change during the play – they **develop**;
- **drama** means 'tension' – often **conflict** between characters;
- **spoken language:** we find out what is happening in plays by **what the characters say,** and we often have to **read between the lines** in order to understand a situation. Plays also use spoken language which can, for example, include **slang** and other **informal ways of speaking**.

c Poems and songs

Important features of a **poem**:

- **structure and rhyme scheme:** most poems are divided into **verses** (also called 'stanzas') and many (but by no means all) **rhyme.** How the **lines** of a poem rhyme is called its **rhyme scheme** and it is described with letters. A rhyme scheme *a-b-a-b* means that the first line rhymes with the third, and the second line with the fourth;

- **poetic language:** poems are generally short compared to stories and plays, but the writer (the **poet)** wants to say a lot in a few lines. To do this, he or she often uses language in a very special way so that the words have a **strong effect** on the reader. There are usually lots of **rhetorical devices** (▶ 4.2), and **images** are particularly important in poems.

Important features of a **song**:

- Songs can be studied as texts like a poem, but remember that the **music** adds a dimension to a song which is not found in a poem;
- **structure** and **rhyme scheme.** Most songs are divided into **two main parts: verses** and **a chorus.** Each verse is **generally different**, however, the chorus **stays the same and is repeated between the verses**. The chorus often contains the **'message'** of the song because listeners hear it several times. Songs can also contain three other parts: **an intro** (at the beginning), a **bridge** (a short part that is neither the verse nor the chorus; it is normally sung only once and contains a new idea in the song), an **outro** (usually very like the intro, but at the end; many songs **fade out** with an outro);
- **poetic language:** songs are also characterised by the special language they use (see poems above).

▶ 3 Understanding a text

The first task you normally have to do on a text is to show that you understand it: you have to do a **comprehension task.** These are the important aspects.

▶ 3.1 Read and understand the text

Texts can be read in three different ways:

Skimming	This means reading **for a quick, general understanding** – often called **reading for gist**. Read through as quickly as you can, concentrating simply on building up a picture of the text in your mind. Do not worry about unknown words.
Scanning	This means reading **to find specific information.** You do this when you look at a railway timetable or a holiday brochure. Make sure you have a clear idea **before you read** of the information you need, and let your eyes move over the text until you find the place where you think it is. Then look closely at that part.
Reading for detail	This is what you do most often when you study a text in order to answer detailed questions on it. The **key steps** are very important. Essentially, you must begin by understanding the **text generally** (skimming). Look at **headlines** and **pictures** that give you an idea about what the text is **about**. Find the overall **structure** of the text as this helps a great deal in understanding what the writer says. NOTE: Do not, at this stage, worry about unknown words. Read again. Still **do not look up words in a dictionary**. Try to work out **(deduce)** as far as you can what unknown words mean from the **context** – the sentence as a whole and the words around the unknown word. Think of other words that are **like** the unknown word (for example, another word in the same **word family**). There may be words in other languages that can help you, too. Finally, if you are still not sure, then you can use your dictionary.

▶ 3.2 Do the task on the text

'NO COPYING!' rule: Never copy directly from a text in summaries or when answering questions!

a **Make a summary**

Many tasks ask you to **sum up / summarise the text** or **outline the main points of the text.** This means that you have to **write a summary of the text as a whole.** These are the important aspects of writing a summary:

- A summary contains all the important information in the original text, but is shorter: normally a summary should **never be longer than 1/2 of the original**.
- The most common tense to use in a summary is the **simple present**.
- **Use your own words.** Do *not* copy from the text!
- Do not use **direct speech**. Report any important words spoken in **indirect speech**.

b **Sum up a specific element of a text**

The task on a text can also be to **find and point out particular parts.** In an argumentative text, this could, for example, be the writer's arguments 'for' something (arguments 'against' are not relevant), or you may be asked to sum up a particular part of a story. Write your summary as described above, but be very careful to **answer the question.** Any other information you include is irrelevant and makes your answer confusing and inaccurate.

▶ 4 Analysing a text

▶ 4.1 Communicating with texts

Analysing texts (**text analysis)** is an important new skill for you and it is helpful to begin by understanding how we communicate generally, and then look specifically at how we **communicate with texts.** These are illustrated by the diagram on the left.

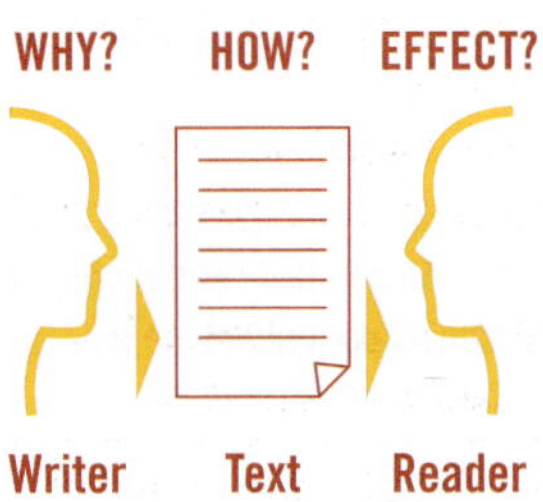

- We can think of all communication as 'sending a message'. Person A (left) sends a message to person B (right).
- The message can be of many kinds – spoken or written. When we communicate with texts, the message takes the form of a written text.
- When we analyse a text, we look at it to answer the questions: **Why** does the writer write the text? **How** does he / she write it? What is the **effect** on the reader?

a **Why?**

What is the writer's **intention (goal)** when writing the text? (to inform? persuade? move emotionally?)

b **How?**

How does the writer write the text so as to achieve his / her goal? For example:

- the **text type** the writer chooses (fictional, non-fictional, informative, ...);
- the **structure** of the text (parts, paragraphs, headlines, ...);
- the **language** the writer uses (formal, informal, poetic, ...) and special **devices** (ways of using language) like **images** in the text or **repeating certain words**.

c **Effect?**

Every technique a writer uses has an effect on the reader, and it is an important part of analysing a text to **explain what the effect is**. For example:

- the **text type** the writer chooses may be **familiar to** the reader, so that he or she has an idea before reading of roughly **what to expect**;

- the **structure** of the text may **make it easier** for the reader, **to follow the writer's thoughts**;
- the **language** the writer uses may make a certain **impression on the reader.** For example, detailed or scientific language in an encyclopedia makes the reader feel the information is accurate and that he / she can **trust the writer**;
- **special devices**, especially in fictional texts, can have a very **strong emotional effect** on the reader, making the text seem amusing, dramatic, shocking, …

▸ 4.2 Rhetorical devices

When you analyse a text, you may be asked to **point out any rhetorical devices used by the writer.** These are special ways of using language and are particularly common in **speeches** and **most fictional texts.** Several of the terms come from Greek or Latin.

Alliteration	Repeating a sound (usually a consonant) at the beginnings of words that are next to each other. The effect is to make e.g. a line of poetry more interesting and beautiful as language: *(Imagine all the people)* ***living life*** *in peace.*
Antithesis	Putting two ideas close together so that there is a clear contrast. The effect is to emphasise just how different the two ideas are: *If you don't know how to fix it, stop breaking it!*
Exaggeration (Hyperbole)	Making a person, action, etc. seem bigger or more important than in reality. The effect is to emphasise something (often in an amusing way): *I am so tired I could sleep for a year!*
Imagery	Expressing an idea through an image – a **mental picture**. It allows the reader / listener to 'see' an **abstract idea** in a concrete way, and so understand it better: *His face was* ***like a red tomato****; I'm* ***drowning in a sea of*** *problems.*
Repetition	There are two main ways in which writers repeat words or phrases in a text. Both (a) help to structure a list of ideas, and (b) emphasise key ideas: - **at the beginning of a sentence** or **part of a sentence (anaphora):** ***It was*** *the best of times,* ***it was*** *the worst of times,* ***it was*** *the age of wisdom,* ***it was*** *the age of foolishness.* - **at the end of a sentence** or **part of a sentence (epiphora):** *here a* ***cousin****, there a* ***cousin,*** *everywhere we turned a kissing* ***cousin*** *was puckering up at us.*
Rhetorical questions	Asking a question to which everyone already knows the answer. In speeches, this is a way of saying something with strong effect: *Do you want war? Do you want hunger in the world? Do you want injustice?* (The clear answer is: *No!*)
Understatement (Litotes)	Making a person, action, situation, etc. seem smaller / less important than in reality (see 'Exaggeration' above). The effect is, in fact, to show just the opposite – how big or important something is: *(Captain of a plane that is about to crash) "Ladies and gentlemen, we have a small problem."*

▶ 4.3 Examples of text analysis

The table below shows four typical examples of text analysis.

Text	Why?	How?	Effect
Poem	The poet wants to express a strong personal feeling to the reader.	- The poem is divided into verses and rhymes. - There are strong images. - Words and phrases are repeated (rhetorical device).	- The reader can follow the ideas and rhymed lines stand out. - The reader 'sees' the ideas more clearly. - The key message of the poem stays in the reader's mind.
Newspaper news article	The journalist wants to give facts about a news event so that the reader finds the article interesting and informative.	- The article has a headline and a photo. - The article is divided into paragraphs. - The journalist explains difficult facts / terms.	- Catches the reader's attention and gives an idea of the story. - The reader follows the information better. - The reader understands the background to the story.
Advertisement	The advertiser wants to sell a new car.	- A large part of the ad is a photo of the car on a beautiful mountain road. - Text explains some technical information. - Ad gives a website / phone number to contact.	- Catches the reader's attention and gives an idea of 'beauty' (and maybe 'freedom'). - Many car enthusiasts love technical detail. The information may also emphasise that the car is economical, etc. – this influences the reader to buy to save money. - Reader can act, find out more / buy the car.
Blog	The blogger wants to express an opinion about something and invite discussion. Readers are generally well-educated.	- Headline, picture and layout. - 'Argumentative' text type. - Links to other pages. - Comment box at the end.	- Catches the reader's attention. - Intelligent readers prefer thought-out opinions and so read. - The reader can choose to look in more detail if he / she chooses. - Encourages the reader to reply and join in a discussion.

▶ 5 Reacting to a text

▶ 5.1 Classroom discussions

In classroom work you are often asked to discuss a text you have read.

- Don't be afraid to try! 'With hands and feet' is also a way of getting ideas across!
- Use the phrases on the inside cover of your book. They give your sentences a structure.
- Learn how to agree and disagree with other students **politely**. This is very important for native speakers of English. You will seem 'German' if, in real conversations later, you are too direct and **abrupt**.

▶ 5.2 Written tasks

a Writing skills: general

Step 1: Plan

- It is almost impossible to write a good text if you are trying to do two things at the same time: (1) work out your ideas and (2) write a text in English. Before you begin writing, therefore, you should **plan – know what you want to say**.
- One way is to **make notes.** Make these **in English.** Making notes in German and then translating them afterwards into English does not work. **Be brief.** Your aim is not to write a text but rather to collect key words and ideas. The only person who has to understand your notes is *you* – you can turn them later into full sentences.
- Another good way to plan is with a **mindmap.**

MINDMAPPING

- **Mindmaps** help you to **collect** and **plan** ideas ready for a writing (or speaking) task. You can make them alone or in a group.
- Draw a flat circle in the middle of a piece of paper and write into it the **central theme** of your mindmap (ADOLESCENCE, WORLD PROBLEMS, NEWS, ...).
- Around this, in smaller circles, arrange the **main aspects** of the theme. For ADOLESCENCE that could be: family life, careers, relationships, problems, etc.
- Thinking then of each aspect at a time, add ideas, key words and expressions connected to each.

Step 2: Develop good writing habits

- Every time you write a text, think of the key things which produce a good text and try to make them part of your writing style.
- Don't use the same sentence structures every time – use relative pronouns, connectors and other grammatical devices to produce **interesting sentences**.
- Don't repeat the same words over and over again – try to **vary how you express things**;
- Build up a **bank of useful expressions** and phrases that you can use to give your sentences a structure
- Divide the text into **paragraphs** so that the ideas are **clear** and connect them **logically**.

- **Remember your reader**. Help him or her to follow your thoughts with **'signals'** in the text, for example: *I would like to begin by discussing … / I would now like to go on to examine … / This point is the most important of all: … / We can illustrate this with the following example: … / In conclusion, therefore, we can say that …*

Step 3: Be accurate

When you are in the middle of writing a text, it is often easy to forget even very simple grammar, spellings, etc. Sometimes you make mistakes because you are not sure of a grammar point. But, more often, you know it, but do not use it accurately because **you do not think.** You *must* learn to write accurately for your exam. Try to avoid mistakes while you are writing your text, but most of all, think of Step 4 below …

Step 4: Check (then check again)

Checking over what you have written is one of the most important steps in producing a good text.

- Concentrate on the text just as a piece of English and go through it several times.
- Read it as if for the first time – as your teacher will, for example.
- Read critically – look hard for mistakes. (Tell yourself: 'There are some!')
- Look particularly at language where you have made mistakes before. Most people make the same mistakes many times.
- When you correct your text, make sure the correction is clear and that your reader knows what the final version is.

b Writing a comment

A typical task is often to **comment** on a text you have read – for example, on a website. Often the comment is a **reply to the writer**:

- Say what you are commenting on: *I am writing about your post on your blog about / I was interested in what you said in your last post about … and would like to tell you some of my ideas;*
- Give your personal opinions using 'I';
- Give your personal opinion using 'I' and back up (justify) your answer saying exactly where and why you agree or disagree with the writer. Make sure your arguments are clear and logical:
  I quite agree with what you said about X because …
  I can't agree with you (I'm afraid) because …
  As I see it, … My reasons are as follows …

c Writing a letter to the editor

Readers can react to newspaper and magazine (or e-zine) articles by writing a **letter to the editor**:

- These letters are much like a **comment** (see above) – they begin by saying **what you are writing about** *(your article about … in your newspaper on* [date] …), and **agree / disagree** with the article and **express your personal viewpoint**. Be **polite and formal** in your letter;
- **Begin** with *Dear Sir;*
- **Sign your letter** with your name and the town / country where you live.

d Writing a review

When you react to a fictional text – a short story, for example – you may be asked to **write a review** (e.g. for a school magazine):

- Begin with a **quick summary** of the story – say (in the simple present) what happens in it.
- **Give your opinion.** Say what was good and so why you liked the text – or what was not so good and so why you did not like it. Include plenty of **examples** from the story to illustrate your viewpoint.
- At the end, you can give the text a **rating** (often done with 'stars'), and either **recommend** it to your readers *(You should definitely read this story)* or **not recommend** it *(Do not waste your time with this story!)*.

e **Creative writing**

After reading a text you may be asked to react to it with a piece of **creative writing**. Some typical examples could be:
- re-telling a story from the point of view of one of the characters in it;
- writing a poem;
- writing a newspaper article about an event in the text you read;
- writing a diary or report in which you imagine an experience you have had.

The following steps can help you with your creative writing:
- Think about the **type of text** you have to write – a diary, a story, etc. Use the **style and features** that are typical of this kind of writing. There is usually some **model** that you can follow when you have to do a task like this – often the text you have just read and are reacting to.
- Think about your **readers** (young or older? people you know or do not know?). This shapes the text you write.
- In a **free writing task** (one where you can **invent the details, characters** etc.), it often helps to **brainstorm** ideas, especially in a group.
- As always, check your writing afterwards for mistakes and ways to improve its logic and structure (▶ 5.2 Step 4).

Sound and (moving) images

▶ 1 Listening

▶ 1.1 Listening for gist

The first task with a listening text is generally to get a **general understanding** of the text – to **listen for gist.**
- Listen right through without worrying about understanding every word. Get a general picture of what is being said and of the overall **structure** of the listening text: a conversation, interview, podcast, scene with several people, voice telling a story, …
- Listen to **how** the voices are speaking and any **background** or **context**. What feelings and emotions are behind the words? What is happening while people are speaking?

- Usually, you want to **note down** or **sum up** what you have heard, and it is best to do this **after you have listened**. First write down just key words or phrases, then develop your notes in more detail, or organise them into a short text.

▶ 1.2 Listening for detail: taking notes

The practical problem when you listen for detail in a text is often that you have to listen **and at the same time take notes**:

- Don't write whole sentences. Note down key words and phrases only. The important thing is that *you* can understand your notes afterwards;
- Use **abbreviations** and **numbers**, for example:

and	+	is	=
and so / therefore	⟶ or >	is not	≠
very	v.	about / roughly	≈
and so on	etc.	twenty-five years	25 yrs.
for example	e.g.	half / three quarters	½ ¾

- With many listening tasks you can develop a **listening grid** (after you have listened for gist and before you listen for detail). You can write notes into this as you listen:

WHO?	*interviewer = Peter Smith / interviewee = Karen*
WHY?	*K went round world by train + ship*
WHEN?	*last yr / Jan-Oct*
HIGHLIGHTS?	*China / S. America / Australia – all v. interesting*
PROBLEMS?	*ill in Tibet / lost money in France*
LEARNED?	*be independent / slow down!*
PLANS?	*work camp next yr in Chile*

▶ 2 Pictures

You are often asked to describe a picture and say what effect it has on the viewer. These are the important aspects to consider:

a **Who? What? Where?**
- Describe the people and where they are **(the setting)** …
- Use the **present continuous** to describe what is happening (▶ Grammar you can use 1.2);
- Say **where in the picture** you can see certain things: in the foreground, in the background, at the top (of the picture), at the bottom (of the picture), on the left / right, in the centre (of the picture)
- Some parts of the picture may be **in (sharp) focus**, others **out of focus (blurred)**.

b **The message?**
- What image / idea / feeling does the picture convey? What is its 'message'?
- How does it convey this message? For example: which is the most important element in the picture? how do the setting / colours, etc. emphasise certain ideas? is the picture dark / bright / colourful / frightening / dramatic / full of action / quiet and calm?

▶ 3 Film and video (moving images)

When you watch a film, you need to use your listening skills (above). However, the essential characteristic of video and film is that it is **a medium which uses moving images to tell the story**. This means learning to 'read' how these images work. The main tool used by video and film makers to tell their story is the **camera**. In addition, they can also use **sound** (**music** or **'voiceovers'**, for example) to add certain effects. On the following pages, you can see the different **shots** ('Einstellungen'), **angles** ('Kamerawinkel') and **camera movements** ('Bewegungen') that **directors** regularly use - and why - and some other **important elements of film and video making techniques**.

▶ 3.1 Camera angles

SHOT	EXAMPLE	WHAT THE SHOT DOES
aerial shot ('Luftaufnahme,' 'Vogelperspektive')		Also sometimes called a **bird's eye shot**, this shows a scene from high in the air (in some cases even from above the Earth itself). Its main function is to show the viewer where the events in the film are happening. This is often called an **establishing shot**.
eye-level shot ('auf Augenhöhe')		Films are mostly about people (the **characters**): what they do and what happens to them. In the real world, we see things like this at **eye level** (at the level of our eyes). In a movie, the eye level shot is also the **normal** way to show the story.
high angle shot ('aufsichtige Einstellung')		The camera can, however, be above (or below) characters and events, and this creates a particular **effect.** Filming from above often gives the impression that the person in the scene is somehow **'small': less important** than other characters or, as in this example, **afraid and worried**.
low angle shot ('untersichtige Einstellung', 'Froschperspektive')		This shot has the opposite effect to a high angle shot. Seen from below, a character can seem **'large': more important** than others, and as in this example **dangerous and threatening. 'Brave'** characters are also often filmed with a low angle shot to make us **admire them**.

▶ 3.2 Camera distances

SHOT	EXAMPLE	WHAT THE SHOT DOES
extreme long shot ('super totale Einstellung')		Extreme long shots are almost always outside and show the **place where the scene is happening**. They are another kind of **establishing shot**. In this shot we can also just see the main character in the scene – an empty street in a cowboy town in the Wild West.
long shot ('totale Einstellung')		Long shots (also called **full shots** or **wide shots**) show **a whole person (or people).** They show the character(s) and the scene they are part of.
medium shot ('halb nahe / halb totale Einstellung')		A medium shot (or **mid shot**) shows more of the character: the **upper part of the character's body** from roughly the knees or hips up. Shots like these are good at showing **what the character is doing** and some of his or her **body language**.
close-up ('Großaufnahme')		Close-ups are one of the most important shots in films and videos. Longer shots show us where the character is, but close-ups almost always show us the character's **face** and his or her **facial expressions:** what the character **is feeling and thinking** at that moment.
extreme close-up ('Detailaufnahme')		As the German word 'Detailaufnahme' tells you, an extreme close-up shows a **small detail** – here the character's eyes. These shots are **extremely dramatic** and the viewer feels very **close to the character**.

▶ 3.3 Two shots

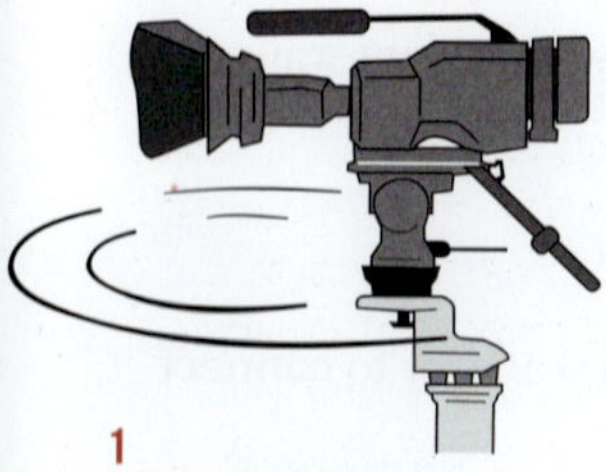

1

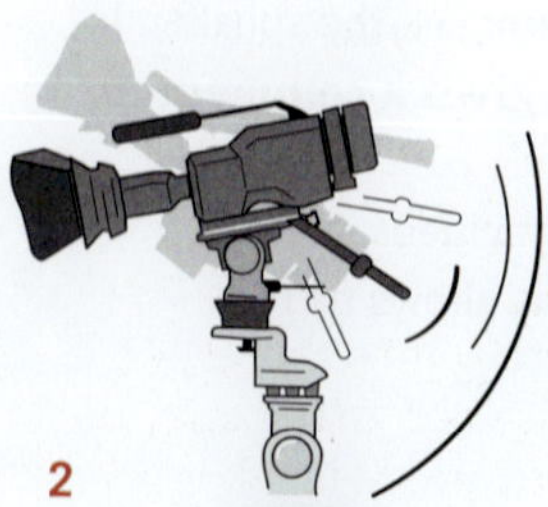

2

3

SHOT	EXAMPLE	WHAT THE SHOT DOES
two shot ('Einstellung mit 2 Personen')		A two shot is any shot in which there are **two characters** (there are also three shots, four shots, etc.). Usually medium shots, two shots very often show **a conversation**. We can see both characters from the front or, as here, both characters from the side.
over the shoulder shot ('über die Schulter Einstellung')		Very often when the scene in a film is a conversation, we see the face of one character (A) **over the shoulder of the second** (B). This allows the viewer to see clearly what A is **thinking and feeling during the conversation**.
reaction shot ('Gegeneinstellung')		In a reaction shot, the camera now goes round to the other side of the conversation and we see **how character B reacts.**

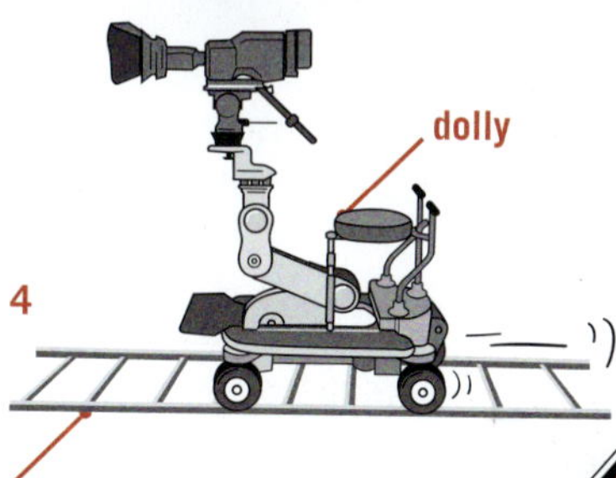

4

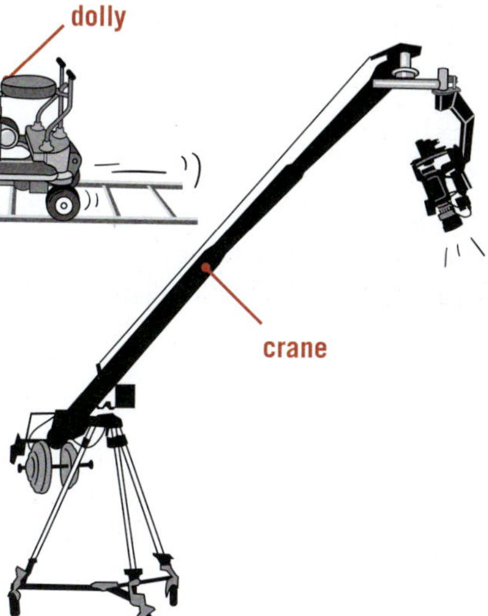

5

▶ 3.4 Camera movements

In most scenes in a movie, the director does not move the camera to shoot a scene – the camera is **static** and the shots are **static shots**. From time to time, though, and for certain effects, the camera can move.
1 **pan / panning shot** ('Schwenk'). The camera moves from side to side – e.g. to show a large scene.
2 **tilt** ('vertikaler Schwenk'). The camera moves up and down.
3 **zoom in** ('Ranfahrt') **/ Zoom out** ('Wegfahrt'). A character, scene, etc. seems to get closer or farther away.
4 **tracking shot** ('Mitschwenk' / 'Fahrt'). The camera on the **dolly** moves with a character (often on a **track**).
5 **crane shot.** a crane can show a scene from above – and move with a character, car, etc.

▶ 3.5 Other video and film techniques

Film and video makers use other techniques, too. Below are a few important ways in which they tell their story in films, documentaries, etc.

a **Sound**

Sound techniques include:
- **background music:** usually to **create an atmosphere** in a scene, or to **connect different scenes**;
- **voiceover** ('Stimme aus dem Off'): we hear a voice, but do not see the speaker. In video documentaries and news programmes the voice often **gives a commentary** on what we are watching;
- **off-screen questions:** sometimes in news and documentary videos, an interviewer that we do not see on screen asks questions. This allows us to concentrate on the interviewee.

b **Visual details**

Film and video makers tell their story through moving images. This means that they often give the viewer information with **visual details**. There are many different kinds, for example:
- We see a plane flying over very low, and know we must be near an airport;
- A quick shot (**cutaway shot** 'Zwischenschnitt') shows us an object, detail, etc. that **helps us to understand the action**;
- We see an American flag on a flagpole near a house. This tells us we are in the USA (and maybe that Americans are patriotic people).

c **Lighting**

How light or dark a scene is adds a lot to the **atmosphere** of the film. Think of all those **horror movies** in which terrible things happen in a dark, old house!

Working in groups and on projects

▶ 1 Making a report to the class

You are often asked to report your group's ideas to the class after doing a task:
- Every member of the group should be able to make the report. Don't leave it always to the same students. If possible, arrange it so that more than one student gives your group report – each one reporting on a different aspect of your ideas.
- Don't write a text and read it aloud. Make notes and use these to help you to speak spontaneously.
- Think of your listeners: put forward your ideas logically; explain difficult words you have used; sum up at the end to emphasise the main points again.
- Ask for questions and be ready to answer them.

▶ 2 Explaining your ideas to other students

In some classroom activities, you have to explain ideas to a student from another group, or to students in your own group.

- Do this by talking, not by showing your notes. The aim of the task is to practise speaking.
- Allow the person / people listening plenty of time to take notes and answer any questions they have about things which are not clear.
- At the end, ask your listener(s) to repeat back to you what they understood. There may be things that are not quite right.

▶ 3 Project work

Project work is normally done in small groups. The project may be to find information and present it to the class, or to make a poster, leaflet, etc.

- Work first as a group and brainstorm ideas (▶ Activity chest 2). Get a clear plan of how you are going to organise your project.
- Divide up the work so that each member of the group has her / his own clear task.
- Set times when each task should be ready – the project will not work if one member of the group is not finished on time. It is a good idea to choose one student who keeps an eye on how the project is going.

▶ 4 Making a formal presentation

In most cases, at the end of a project, you have to present it to the class – you have to make a formal presentation. These are the basic rules for a good presentation.

RULES FOR A SUCCESSFUL PRESENTATION
- If you have worked in a group, decide exactly **who gives your presentation**. Presentations usually work best if more than one person speaks. - **Use 'visuals'**. It is a fact that we receive 80 per cent of information through our eyes and only 20 per cent through our ears. Help your listeners with an overhead projector or large piece of paper on which you list main points and show diagrams or pictures to help them to take in what you say. - Don't write a text and simply read it aloud. **Speak from notes** and sound spontaneous. - **Speak slowly and loudly**. Talk to the students at the back of the class. - **Look at your listeners**. Eye contact is important. - **Structure your talk clearly**. People in business who frequently make presentations always say that you should: • **'Tell the audience what you are going to say'**: *I (we) would like to speak today about … / I will begin by … then I will go on to look at … / Finally, I will ….* • **'Say it'**: give the main part of your presentation. Again, help the audience as much as possible to follow your ideas with phrases such as: *OK, I have spoken about …. I would now like to go on to … / The next main point I want to make is … / I would like to turn now to …* • **'Tell the audience what you have said'**: sum up your main points with phrases such as *That brings me to the end of my talk, and I would like just to sum up the main points / To sum up, then, …* - Most presentations normally end with a chance for the listeners to **ask questions.** You can invite them to do this with a phrase such as: *Thanks for listening. Now, are there any questions?*

Grammar you can use

▶ 1 Verbs

▶ 1.1 The simple present

Use the simple present:

- to talk and write about texts, videos and films:
  This text is about …
  In this scene we learn that …
  The filmmakers want to create the effect that …
- in summaries:
  At first, the family lives in New York, but they soon move to Los Angeles.
- to talk and write about all facts, situations, etc. that are true generally and for a long time. This often happens when you give statistics:
  Around 15 per cent of all Americans are Hispanics. Most live in the south of the USA.
- with adverbs like *sometimes, often, regularly, usually, normally, always, frequently, never*: *We usually go to Turkey for our summer holidays – and it is often pretty boring!*

Watch out for …

- 'Nach *he/she/it* das 'S' muss mit!: *I live – you live – we live –they live.*
  BUT! He/she/it ***lives***.
- In negative sentences, use *does* after *he/she/it*. But don't put 'S' on the main verb: *She doesn't **live**. (~~lives~~)*
- There's is no 'S' on the main verb in questions either: *Does he **live**? (~~lives~~)*

▶ 1.2 The present progressive (continuous)

Use the present progressive:

- for any action that is happening right now – for example, a scene in a video:
  Two people are standing near a car. They are talking. In the background, the sun is shining.
- to describe a trend that you can see at the moment:
  Today, more and more people are travelling abroad on business.

Watch out for …

- Don't forget to include *be*: *They are returning from abroad at the moment. (~~They returning~~ from abroad at the moment.*
- Be careful of the spellings of the -ing forms. For example: *sit / sitting; make / mak(e)~~ing~~*. If you are not sure, check in your dictionary.
- These verbs are not normally used in the present progressive: *be, come from* ('stammen aus'), *have* ('besitzen', 'verfügen über'), *know, like, hate, think* ('der Meinung sein'), *want*.

▶ 1.3 Simple past and present perfect

Use the simple past:

- to tell a story:
  Trudi opened the door and went into the kitchen. She took a carton of orange from the fridge, poured some juice into a glass, and sat down at the kitchen table.
- for events in the past that happened one after another:
  It was a company called 'Nestor' that opened Hollywood's first film studio. Soon, more studios opened along Hollywood boulevard. Within three years, the whole street had banks, restaurants, cinemas and clubs – all to support this new industry.
- with past time expressions (years, dates, centuries, etc.):
  In the 16th century, Spain was the world's biggest sea power. In 1521, it conquered Mexico. Spain's first settlement in America was in 1565, when the Spanish founded the town of St. Augustine in Florida.

Watch out for ...

- Many verbs have an irregular form in the past. You can find lists of these in a dictionary.
- Be careful with negative sentences and questions: *I didn't go (I didn't ~~went~~) Did he go? (Did he ~~went~~?)*

Use the present perfect:

- with *for* (+ a period of time), and *since* (+ a point in time):
  They have lived here for 10 years. She has been a German citizen since 2004.
- for things that have happened recently ('neulich', 'in letzter Zeit'). Newspaper articles often begin with the present perfect like this:
  Scientists have discovered a new planet.
  A new report has shown that three billion people worldwide now use the internet.

Watch out for ...

- Many verbs have an irregular past participle ('3. Form'). You can find lists of these in a dictionary.
- Don't automatically use the present perfect for German expressions like: 'Ich habe gestern einen guten Film gesehen'. Most of the time, these verbs will be in the simple past in English.

▶ 1.4 *Will* and *going to*

Use *will*:

- for events in the future that you know, think or hope will happen:
  By 2050, half the population of the world will speak English.
  I think my work placement in London will be very exciting.

Use *going to*:

- to talk about plans for things in the future ('was Sie oder jemand vorhat'):
  Next year, my family and I are going to emigrate to Australia.
- for something that is about to happen very soon ('gleich'):
  You are going to read a text from a British website.

▶ 1.5 Conditional sentences

Use conditional sentences to speculate about events in the future, and to look back at events in the past. The key word in all conditional sentences is *if* ('Was passiert, wenn ...?', 'Was würde passieren, wenn ...?', 'Was wäre passiert, wenn ...?').

Conditional sentences Type 1

- If A happens (or doesn't happen), B will be certain:
  If we don't cut our carbon emissions, the Earth will get warmer.
  IF + SIMPLE PRESENT, WILL ...

Conditional sentences Type 2

- 'What if ...?' things we imagine:
  If I was one of the characters in the story, I would be very afraid.
  IF + SIMPLE PAST, WOULD ...

Conditional sentences Type 3

- This is about events in the past. Usually, they are events that didn't happen, and we think about 'Was wäre passiert, wenn ...?':
  If people 100 years ago had known about global warming (but they didn't), maybe they would have been more careful about things like burning so much coal.
  IF + PAST PERFECT, WOULD HAVE ...

Watch out for ...

- Never use *would* in Conditional 2 sentences twice: *If I lived in England, I would speak English. (If I ~~would live~~ in England, ...)*

▶ 1.6 Modal verbs

a **May, might, could** ('Möglichkeit')

Use *may, might* and *could* to talk about possibility:

This news story may be true or it may not. (50 % chance)

The story might / could be true – but personally, I don't think it is. (10 %-20 % chance).

b **Have to, don't have to (needn't), mustn't** ('Notwendigkeit')

Use *have to, don't have to (needn't),* and *mustn't* to talk about necessity:

You have to be careful when they use the internet. It can be dangerous. ('müssen')

Students mustn't use their mobile phones in class. ('nicht dürfen')

I get free text messaging – I don't have to / needn't pay for texting. ('nicht müssen')

Watch out for ...

German and English use *mustn't* and 'muss nicht' in different ways:

You mustn't do that = Sie dürfen das nicht tun.

You don't have to / needn't come to school in the holidays. = Sie müssen nicht in den Ferien zur Schule kommen.

▶ 1.7 Reported speech

You can report what someone says or thinks with reported speech. To do this, you use a reporting verb such as: *say, tell, answer, emphasise, admit*. You can use *that* or leave it out.

a **Reported speech with a present tense reporting verb**

Use reported speech with a present tense reporting verb in a summary. The tenses of the original words and thoughts stay the same:

TEXT: "We now have over 500 members of our school Bike Club and I think this number will grow next year."

SUMMARY: *The writer tells us in his blog that there are now more than 500 people in the Bike Club and that he believes there will be even more next year.*

b **Reported speech with a past tense reporting verb**

Use reported speech with a past tense reporting verb in reports and to write newspaper articles. The tenses of the original words and thoughts change as follows:

Original words / thoughts ("...")	**Reported speech (She said ...)**
Simple present: "The camp is our home!"	Simple past: *the camp was their home.*
Present progressive: "We are fighting to save our homes."	Past progressive: *they were fighting to save their homes.*
Simple past: "We came here last year."	Past perfect: *they had come there the year before.*
Present perfect: "Many people have left recently."	Past perfect: *many people had left recently.*
Will Future: "We will stay here."	*Would*: they would stay there.

Watch out for ...

Say and *tell* are used differently:

The president ***told us*** */ reporters / his listeners that he was very worried about world terrorism. (~~The president told that he ...~~)*

The president ***said (that)*** *he was very worried about world terrorism. (The president ~~said us / reporters etc.~~) that ...*

▶ 1.8 Verbs + infinitive, verbs + gerund (-ing)

It is often necessary to use two verbs one after the other. Sometimes the second verb must be an infinitive, sometimes it must be a gerund. After a few verbs, the second verb can be an infinitive or a gerund with no big difference in meaning. On the next page you can see which verbs are used in which ways.

a **Verbs + infinitive**

Use the infinitive (with *to*) after these verbs, e.g. *We agreed to meet at 8 o'clock:*

agree	vereinbaren	*manage*	es schaffen
arrange	abmachen	*(not) need*	(nicht) brauchen
attempt	versuchen	*offer*	anbieten
afford	sich leisten können	*plan*	vorhaben
choose	vorziehen, sich entscheiden	*promise*	versprechen
decide	sich entscheiden	*refuse*	sich weigern
expect	erwarten	*seem*	scheinen
fail	es nicht schaffen	*want*	wollen
learn	lernen	*wish*	wünschen
hope	hoffen	*I would like*	Ich würde gern

b **Verbs + gerund**

Use the gerund after these verbs, e.g. *We enjoy watching films:*

avoid	vermeiden	*imagine*	sich vorstellen
can't help	nicht anders können als	*miss*	vermissen
dislike	nicht mögen	*practise*	üben
enjoy	genießen	*risk*	riskieren
finish	beenden	*stop*	aufhören
go on	fortfahren	*suggest*	vorschlagen

c **Verbs + infinitive or gerund**

Use either the infinitive or the gerund after these verbs, e.g. *We began reading together / We began to read together:*

begin	beginnen	*love*	lieben
continue	fortfahren	*intend*	die Absicht haben
hate	hassen	*prefer*	vorziehen
like	mögen	*start*	anfangen

▶ 1.9 Gerund after expressions

There are several useful expressions that you can use when talking and writing which are all followed by the gerund:

- *by* + gerund ('indem …'). This expressions explains how something is done and is particularly useful in text analysis:
  The writer conveys this idea to his readers by using imagery and a number of clever rhetorical devices.
- *there is no point in / it is no good* ('es hat keinen Zweck') / *it is (not) worth it* ('es lohnt sich (nicht)') + gerund:
  There is no point in speculating about this – we simply have no idea.
  It is worth pointing out that the writer's view is highly unusual.

▶ 1.10 The passive

Use the passive when you write informative or argumentative texts to make your text more formal and authoritative ('verlässlich'). The passive exists in all tenses and there is a passive infinitive. The table below shows the main passive forms.

Simple present	*energy is produced (by the sun)*
Present progressive	*energy is being produced*
Simple past	*energy was produced*
Will future	*energy will be produced*
Going to future	*energy is going to be produced*
Conditional 2	*energy would be produced*
Infinitive	*energy can be produced*

Watch out for ...

The word 'von' in German conditional sentences is *by* in English:
Hamlet was written by Shakespeare (~~from~~ Shakespeare).

▶ 2 Relative clauses

Use relative clauses to make the sentences you write more interesting – for example, by combining two short sentences into one longer one.

▶ 2.1 Relative pronouns

The short words that begin a relative clause are relative pronouns:

- *who* is always used for people;
- *which* is always used for things;
- *that* can be used for both – but is more common for things;
- *whose* has the meaning 'dessen / deren' and can be used for people and things;
- *where* is often used as a relative pronoun in sentences like: *This is the house where I was born.*

▶ 2.2 Relative pronouns as subject and object

The relative pronoun at the beginning of the relative clause in a sentence can be the subject of the clause or the object of it. This produces two quite different types of sentence, and it is important to recognise them:
Subject: *The scientist* ***who has*** *the best ideas about this is Dr Frazer.* (*who* comes directly next to the verb)
Object: *The people* ***who*** *we* ***spoke*** *to about this did not agree.* (another word or expression comes between *who* and the verb).
More examples:
Subject: *The Spanish were the first Europeans* ***who settled*** *in North America.*
Object: *The characters* ***who*** *the writer* ***invents*** *for this story are all very amusing.*
Subject: *This director makes many films* ***which are*** *full of action.*
Object: *The film* ***which*** *he* ***made*** *last year, however, was very different.*

▸ 2.3 Leaving out the relative pronoun (contact clauses)

In sentences where the relative pronoun is the object of the relative clause, you can leave it out and use a contact clause:
Full sentence: All of the scenes **that** we se**e** in the film take place in a taxi.
Contact clause: *All the **scenes we see** in the film take place in a taxi.*
Full sentence: The man **who** they met in Melbourne was a dance teacher.
Contact clause: *The **man they met** in Melbourne was a dance teacher.*

▸ 3 Adjectives and adverbs

Use adjectives and adverbs in texts to make them more colourful and expressive – to tell your reader more about a person, place, event, someone's feeling, how events happen, etc.

▸ 3.1 Adjective or adverb?

- Adjectives describe nouns (people, things etc.) and usually go before the noun or after verbs like *be*, *seem* and *become*:
  It was a very dramatic event. The event was / seemed / became very dramatic.
- Remember that the –ing and –ed forms of verbs are often used as adjectives:
  The writer now makes a surprising remark. We were all surprised when we read it.
- Adverbs of manner ('der Art und Weise') belong together with a verb to give information about how something happens. Almost all end in –ly.
  We drove slowly from the valley up into the mountains.
  When we arrived in the mountain village, the children ran out excitedly to meet us.
- After these verbs you do not use an adverb but an adjective instead: *feel, look, smell, sound, taste*. For example:
  I feel tired. (~~tiredly~~)
  You look nice. (~~nicely~~)
- Adverbs like *extremely*, *totally*, *completely*, and *surpringly* are often used before an adjective:
  It is an extremely difficult decision. (an ~~extreme~~ difficult decision)

Watch out for ...

- There are some spelling rules that you need to be careful about when you add –ly . For example: possible – *possibly*, happy – *happily.* Check in your dictionary if you are not sure.
- A small number of adjectives end in –ly. The two most common are *likely* (= probable) and *friendly*. There is no adverb from likely. For the adverb form of *friendly*, use a phrase like *in a friendly way*.

▸ 3.2 The comparison of adjectives

Use the comparative and superlative forms of adjectives ('Steigerungsformen') to compare things:
The first part of the story is shorter than the second, but in my opinion it is much more exciting.
This is definitely the most biased news story I have ever read.

All short adjectives (1 syllable):	*short – shorter – the shortest*
Adjectives of 2 syllables ending in -er:	*clever – cleverer – the cleverest*
All other adjectives of 2+ syllables:	*exciting – more exciting / less exciting – the most exciting / least exciting*

Watch out for ...

- Remember spelling rules when you make the comparative and superlative forms of short 1-syllable adjectives (big – *bigger*, healthy – *healthiest*, etc.). Check in a dictionary if you are not sure.
- Use *than* after a comparative form: *Hispanics are often poorer than other people in America. (poorer ~~as~~ other people)*

▶ 4 Singular and plural nouns

A whole sequence of your book is about 'news'. *News* is an example of an English noun that looks plural, but is, in fact, singular. Some nouns, on the other hand, look singular but can be plural.

- The nouns *advice, information, mathematics, news, politics, progress, the UN / the United Nations, the USA / the United States* are always singular in English:
  Politics ***is*** *sometimes difficult to understand.*
  The USA ***is*** *the world's most powerful nation at the moment.*
- Some words (collective nouns) are for groups of people: *class* (school), *club, company* (firm), *family, government, team*. These nouns are usually singular:
  The government we have at the moment ***is*** *terrible.*
  The company ***is*** *Germany's biggest producer of electricity.*
  However, they can also be plural if you want to emphasise the individual members of the group:
  Mother, father, children – the family ***are*** *all nice.*
  The team ***are*** *all excited about the next match.*
- *Police* is always plural:
  The police ***are*** *looking for a man aged around 30 with blond hair.*

Check your grammar (answers)

▶ **Page 11**

Exercise 1: b spent / left, **c** was / took, **d** played / compared / got, **e** liked / rushed, f laid, g had / saw
Exercise 2: b Why did they leave next morning? **c** How did the students get to know each other quickly? **d** Why did the students rush into the lecture room? **e** Where did they play cards? **f** What did (the) students learn during the role play?
Exercise 3: a weren't excited, **b** didn't spend / didn't leave, **c** wasn't (by train) / didn't take, **d** didn't play / didn't compare / didn't get

▶ **Page 17**

Exercise 1: a divide, **b** are represented, **c** is spoken, **d** speak, **e** estimate, **f** is estimated
Exercise 2: a English is spoken (by people) in India. **b** English is used as a communication tool by business people. **c** English will be spoken by half the world's population one day. **d** It is often said that English is a difficult language.

▶ **Page 28**

b are you going to do, **c** Are you going to apply, **d** will be, **e** will be, **f** am going to learn, **g** will you live / will have, **h** am going to visit / am also going to go / am going to eat, **i** he will come

▶ **Page 32**

Exercise 1: b have lived, **c** rented / bought, **d** have been, **e** have you been, **f** did you start, **g** did you do / went, **h** has lived
Exercise 2: b harder, **c** better, **d** bigger / big, **e** cold / colder, **f** worse / worst / slowest

▶ **Page 40**

Exercise 1: a live, **b** comes, **c** is, **d** often face, **e** regularly have, **f** usually have, **g** are / live
Exercise 2: a tells, **b** says, can, **c** think / expresses, **d** makes / have / are, **e** is / arrive / murders / travels / is
Exercise 3: b Where are your parents from? **c** Why do you and your sisters hate America? **d** How often do you go back to Central America? **e** What do you do there? **f** How many other people from Central America go to your school?
Exercise 4: b doesn't live, **c** doesn't go, **d** don't live, **e** don't sing, **f** don't get on

▶ **Page 56**

Exercise 1: The place where the story takes place is New York. / The character who makes this decision is Mami. / The sentence which best sums up their attitudes in lines … / The people in the story whose lives we learn most about are the girls. / The houses where the girls live are not as big as they would like. / An example which illustrates this is: "…" / There are lots of girls whose families are all rich and famous.
Exercise 2: b The girls make jokes about the young people who live on the Island. **c** I think it is wrong to criticise people whose lives are just different from ours. **d** In the end, the girls come to hate the place where / in which they were born and grew up.

▶ **Page 67**

Exercise 1: a DJ-ing (to DJ), **b** volunteering (to volunteer), **c** to respect, **d** to get, **e** to build
Exercise 2: a going / going (to go), **b** working / to get, **c** to work, **d** to build, **e** to rent, **f** to listen, **g** to get, **h** to build / to become / sleeping / being

▶ **Page 76**

a is, **b** is / isn't, **c** is, **d** is, **e** is, **f** leads, **g** is, **h** wants, **i** are looking for

▶ **Page 93**

He said that **was** the biggest catastrophe in the history of the Mississippi area. So far 1,476 people **had** died. Thousands more **were** homeless. The disaster **was** so immense that reacting to it **was** an almost impossible task. However, **they were** doing everything **they could** to help people. The army and medical services **were** in the area, and yesterday the government **had set** aside $2 billion dollars to rebuild the area. More help **would** arrive in the next few days. **They would** let **us** have more information as soon as it **was** available.

▶ **Page 115**

Exercise 1: b would have, **c** would have joined, **d** were, **e** had not lost, **f** get, **g** would be, **h** had known / would have behaved

Wordfields

Sequence 1

- abroad / overseas; *go / travel / live ~* - adjust to sth. - applicant - application (letter of ~); *write a(n) ~* - apply for; *~ a job / a placement* - au pair (agency) - cross-cultural / intercultural - culture - culture shock; *experience ~* - emigrate (an emigrant); *~ to a new country* - employ sb. - employee - employer - exchange student - experience; *have a good / bad / interesting ~* - global language - host family; *live with / in a ~* - immigrate / an (illegal) immigrant - impression(s); *get an / the ~ (that)* - intercultural communication	- job advertisement - keep an open mind about sth. - lingua franca; *English is used as a ~* - (national) stereotype - nationality(-ies) - native speaker - official / second language - placement; *find a / have a ~* - realise (a dream) - responsibility; *have (the) ~ for sth.* - rude(ness) / polite(ness) - settle (abroad) - smuggler - the EU - volunteer (n.) - volunteer (v.) - volunteer work - work camp; *attend / take part in a ~* - work placement / internship; *do a(n) ~* - worldwide

Sequence 2

- actor / actress / (film) director / (film) producer - adolescent / adolescence - adult / adulthood / child / childhood - alcohol / alcoholism / drink (n.) - ASBO (Antisocial Behaviour Order) - attitude; *have an ~ towards sth.* - belonging - between two cultures; *grow up ~* - career; *have / choose a ~* - cast (of a film) - Central America - charity (organisation) - conflict; *face / experience ~* - crime / (gun ~ / knife ~) / criminal - depression / despair; *suffer from ~* - disappointed (in sb.); *be ~* - dole (on the ~) / unemployed / unemployment - dream job; *look for / find your ~* - drop out (v.) / dropping out (n.)	- eating disorder; *have an / suffer from an ~* - ethnic minority; *belong to an / be part of an ~* - face a problem / issue - fail; *fail at sth.* - get involved in sth. - Hispanic / Latino / Black / Asian (American) - homeless(ness) - identity; *look for your true ~* - law; *break the ~* - lyrics; *the ~ of a song* - oppression - peer - Pledge of Allegiance; *take the / swear the ~* - politician - relationship; *have a good / bad ~ with …* - role model; *be a ~, choose a ~* - stereotype sb. - suicide; *commit ~ / attempted ~* - take drugs - waste of time / money; *be a ~* - youth club; *belong to a / join a ~*

Sequence 3

- advantage / disadvantage; *~ and ~ of sth.*
- anchorman / -woman
- asylum / asylum seeker
- background (situation)
- biased / unbiased; *the article is ~*
- broadcast (v.) / broadcast (n.)
- catastrophe / disaster / disastrous
- channel (TV ~)
- citizen journalist
- cyberbullying; *be a victim of ~*
- cyberfriend; *have a ~ / meet a ~*
- editor
- elections; *~ take place every four years*
- entertainment
- event
- government *(spelling!)*
- headline / strapline / byline / crosshead / caption / column
- human interest; *a ~ story*
- information *(singular!)*
- journalist / reporter
- latest; *the ~ news*
- leading article (leader)
- media outlet
- news *(singular!); hard ~ / ~ story / ~ category / ~ programme*
- politics *(singular!); be interested in ~*
- privacy
- protest (v.) / protest (n.) / protester
- quality newspaper / tabloid newspaper
- report sth. / report (n.)
- sensational; *a ~ news story / report (about ...)*
- social networking (site); *see sth. on a ~*
- technology / technologies
- terror / terrorist / terrorism
- the (English) Channel
- the (mass / new) media
- threat (be a ~ to sb.)
- trivial; *a ~ news story*
- video footage; *~ of an event*

Sequence 4

- (dis)engaged in sth.
- (make a) speech / speaker; *a ~ about sth.*
- 'pros' and 'cons'; *the ~ of a situation*
- activist; *be / become an ~*
- apathy / apathetic; *feel apathetic about sth.*
- bin; *compost ~, recycling ~, rubbish ~*
- carbon footprint; *reduce your ~*
- characteristic(s); *the ~ of sth.*
- child abuse; *commit / suffer from ~*
- climate change
- CO2 (emissions)
- commitment; *have a (strong) ~ to sth.*
- conservation (authority)
- consumer
- crop(s); *grow / cultivate ~*
- demonstrate / demonstration; *~ about sth.*
- destroy sth. / destruction
- DND (deoxyribonucleic acid)
- eco-label
- environment / environmentalist
- environmental organisation
- equal / equality
- extinct / extinction; *become ~*
- gene / genetic modification / genetically modified (GM) / genetics (science)
- get at the truth
- global warming; *the problem of ~*
- greenwashing; *an example of ~*
- hatred; *show / feel / experience ~*
- initiative; *start an ~ (in a school etc.)*
- make your voice heard
- organic (food)
- participate in sth.
- petition; *sign / start a ~ (about ...)*
- pollution; *cause ~*
- power station; *coal-fired ~*
- poverty; *suffer from / solve the problem of ~*
- rainforest(s); *destroy / conserve / save (the) ~*
- recycle / recycling
- renewable energy; *be a source of ~*
- selective breeding; *use ~*
- side effect; *the ~ of sth.*
- species (of animals, plants)
- Third World
- UN (United Nations)
- war / peace

Acknowledgements

Texts

Sequence 1, pp. 8 - 10: From: Travelogue on RheinAhrCampus, FH Koblenz web-page: (www.rheinahrcampus.de/international/projects/achill2009/travelogue/); p. 13: From: BBC NEWS, 24 October 2001 (http://news.bbc.co.uk/2/hi/talking_point/1617138.stm); **p. 18:** From: SPIEGEL ONLINE International, 18 May 2006 (http://www.spiegel.de/international/0,1518,416920,00.html); **p. 23:** Kristina Bellach / iSt Internationale Sprach- und Studienreisen GmbH (http://www.aupair-erfahrungsberichte.de/aupair_europa/england/greater_london/kristina_bellach_berichtet_aus_london_greater_london__england_one_year_in/); **p. 31:** From: Kabeleins, © 2010 SevenOne Intermedia GmbH (http://www.kabeleins.de/doku_reportage/neues_leben/postkarte/16081/)

Sequence 2, p. 42: Words & Music by Chester Bennington, Mike Shinoda, Rob Bourdon, Joseph Hahn, Brad Delson & David Farrell © Copyright 2003 Big Bad Mr. Hahn Music / Rob Bourdon Music / Kenji Kobayashi Music / Chesterchaz Publishing / Nondisclosure Agreement Music / Pancakey Cakes Music, USA. Imagem Music. Used by permission of Music Sales Limited. All Rights Reserved. International Copyright Secured; **p. 45:** © K. Ari / M. Pegah / El Cerrito High School, California; **pp. 50 - 51, 53 -54:** From: *How the Garcia Girls Lost Their Accents* by Julia Alvarez, © Bloomsbury, London 2004, © original edition 1991 Julia Alvarez; **pp. 65-66:** © The Sun 04 Jun 2008 / nisyndication.com; **pp. 68-69:** 'Needing Love' is taken from the collection *Acting It Out* by Marsh Cassady and Joan Sturkie, © Resource Publications, Inc.(rpinet.com) 1990. All rights reserved. Used by special permission of the publisher; **p. 71:** Anja Gerstberger, Juppidu Magazin 2008 (http://www.juppidu.de/juppidu/interessantes/pubertaet%20ist%20klasse.html)

Sequence 3, p. 78: From: The Independent 21 September 2009 (http://www.independent.co.uk/news/world/europe/french-police-move-on-jungle-migrant-camp-1791074.html); **p. 80:** From: The Independent 23 September 2009 (http://www.independent.co.uk/opinion/leading-articles/leading-article-europe-needs-to-face-up-to-the-migration-challenge-1791642.html); **p. 82:** © The Sun, 24 December 2007 / nisyndication.com (http://www.thesun.co.uk/sol/homepage/news/article616152.ece); **p. 88:** From: The Guardian, 28 January 2010 (http://www.guardian.co.uk/business/2010/jan/28/tesco-bans-shopping-bananas-pyjamas); **p. 89:** From: Metro.co.uk, February 2010 (http://www.metro.co.uk/news/810861-bathwater-saves-haiti-survivor-after-15-days); **p. 96:** From: The Guardian, 16 January 2009 (http://www.guardian.co.uk/media/pda/2009/jan/16/hudson-river-plane-crash-internet); **p. 97:** From: The Times, 29 December 2009 (http://www.timesonline.co.uk/tol/news/world/middle_east/article6969958.ece); **p. 98:** © 2010 Tony Rogers (http://journalism.about.com) Used with permission of About Inc., which can be found online at www.about.com. All rights reserved; **p. 99:** From: Rheinische Post, 12 February 2010 (http://nachrichten.rp-online.de/article/politik/Allein-mit-Twitter-und-Facebook-ein-Experiment/67621); **pp. 101-102:** From: ReadWriteWeb, August 10 2009 (http://www.readwriteweb.com/archives/your_real_friends_are_your_online_friends_or_so_says_gen_y.php); **p. 105:** From a brochure (p. 83) published by Office of the Data Protection Commissioner, Canal House, Station Road, Portarlington, Co. Laois, Ireland

Sequence 4, pp. 108-109: Text by Josephine Khali (http://www.actnow.com.au/Opinion/Are_young_people_political_enough.aspx), The Inspire Foundation (www.inspire.org.au); **p. 110-113:** © Barbara Cervone / WhatKidsCanDo (http://www.whatkidscando.org/); **p. 114-115:** © Bund für Umwelt und Naturschutz Deutschland e.V. (BUND) (http://www.bund.net/bundnet/ueber_uns/bundjugend/); **p. 119-120:** © Mickie / Teen Ink (www.teenink.com); **p. 124:** (top, left to right) Bundesministerium für Umwelt, Naturschutz und Reaktorsicherheit / European Commission, DG Environment / U.S. Environmental Protection Agency; (bottom, left to right) Fairtrade Foundation, London / The Coalition for Consumer Information on Cosmetics, Philadelphia / Rainforest Alliance, New York; **p. 128:** © John Lennon / EMI Music Publishers; **p. 130:** © Trey / Tavern, Delmar Elementary School, Maryland, USA; © Sam, Benjamin Britten High School, Lowestoft; *Dreams*, from THE COLLECTED POEMS OF LANGSTON HUGHES by Langston Hughes, edited by Arnold Rampersad with David Roessel, Associate Editor, © 1994 by the Estate of Langston Hughes. Used by permission of Alfred A. Knopf, a division of Random House, Inc.; **pp. 132-139:** Story from: *Under the Weather Stories About Climate Change,* edited by T. Bradman, © George Ivanoff, Frances Lincoln Children's Books, London 2009

Photos / Illustrations

AFP/Getty Images: p. 97; **Alamy images**: p. 7 (top centre: © Peter Jobst, top right: © Collectiva, bottom left: © MIXA, bottom centre: © rungtip chatadee, bottom right: © Fancy), p. 8 (top right: © Design Pics Inc.), p. 12 (left: © Johnny Greig concepts, right: © Amazing Images), p. 13 (© Westend61 GmbH), p. 14 (top: © Timothy Swope, centre: © GlowImages, bottom: © Andy Ennis), p. 15 (top left: © Andres Rodriguez, top right: © Image Source Black, bottom right: © amana images inc.), p. 16 (left: © Ian Fraser, centre: © GAMUT STOCK IMAGES PVT LTD GAMUT, right: © EIGHTFISH), p. 20 (© Fancy), p. 21 (left: © Helen Rogers, right: © Image Source Black), p. 22 (©Bubbles Photolibrary), p. 25 (centre: © Walter Quirtmair), p. 26 (© Image Source Pink), p. 29 (© Blackout Concepts), p. 39 (B: © Radius Images, C: © Denkou Images, D: © MBI), p. 41 (© Russell Blake), p. 44 (©Luciano Leon), p. 46 (singer: © John Bentley, footballer: © image100, old woman: © Elena Elisseeva, tennis player: © Aspix), p. 48 (bottom: © David Lyons), p. 49 (right: © Aurora Photos), p. 50 (left: © Danita Delimont, right: © ClassicStock), p. 53 (© Somos Images), p. 57 (©Wave Royalty Free), p. 58 (top: © nik wheeler), p. 63 (top left: © Lyndsay Russell, centre: © colinspics, bottom right: © Ray Grover), p. 68 (© Mark Burnett), p. 72 (top: © FancyVeerSet7, bottom: Corbis Premium RF), p. 73 (girl with laptop: © UpperCut Images), p. 84 (© STOCK4B GmbH), p. 86 (top: © david hancock, bottom: © Jim West), p. 90 (top: © Marvin Dembinsky Photo Associates), p. 106 (top: © Chris Knapton), p. 107 (top left: © Stephan Mulcaney, top right: © WORDS AND MEANINGS/MARK SYKES, centre left: © Deco Images II, centre right: © PhotoAlto), p. 116 (top left: © Image Source, top right: © LeWhite), p. 117 (bottom: © Pictorial Press Ltd), p. 123 (top left: © moodboard, top right: © Image Source), p. 125 (India: © Sebastian Wasek), p. 128 (left: © B.A.E. Inc., centre: © Tom Hanley), p. 131 (bottom centre: © amana images inc., dry earth: Chris Pancewicz), p. 134 (bin: © Ian Wood), p. 135 (© Lynch Creative Ltd), p. 137 (© Tony Cordoza); **Anna Brown**, USA: p. 38 (*On her way* ... © 2000); **Bruce Edwards**, New Zealand: p. 108; **Comstock / Corbis**: p. 39 E; **Corbis**: p. 25 (© Sean White/Design Pics), p. 89 (© Daniel More), p. 128 (right: © Bettmann), p. 131 (top centre: © Warren Faidley); **Cross-Cultural Solutions**, New York: p. 24; **D'Arcy Drury / Abu Dhabi Men's College**, UAE: p. 87; **dpa Picture Alliance**: p. 18 (© Ralf Hirschberger / picture-alliance / ZB), p. 48 (top), p. 63 (bottom left), p. 74, p. 77 (top: © OK_DIFFUSION), p. 77 (bottom), p. 98; **Dr Elmar-Laurent Borgmann**, RheinAhrCampus, FH Koblenz: p. 8 (bottom), 9, 10; **Fotolia**: p. 58 (bottom: © nik wheeler); **Getty Images**: p. 8 (top left: © IIC / Axiom), p. 42 (© Tim Mosenfelder), p. 49 (left: © Photodisc); **Hans-Joachim Bloombach**, Herford: p. 6 (bottom); **iStockphoto**: p. 6 (top right: © DanDriedger); **ITN Source**, London: p. 90 (bottom left and right); **ITN Source/ECL:** p. 118 (bottom); **LGP**, Brighton: p. 15 (bottom left: from the *How To Be British Collection* © LGP, Brighton, UK); **Lilen Pautasso**: p. 15 (centre right); **Locus Solus**, New York: p. 59, pp. 61-62 (photo stills from NIGHT ON EARTH © 1991 Locus Solus Inc, All Rights Reserved); **News Team International**, London: p. 65 (© News Team International); **Reuters / Corbis**: p. 96; **Roadtrip Productions**, Costa Mesa, USA: p. 46 (top two images), p. 47; **RWE AG:** p. 123 (bottom left); **Severn Cullis-Suzuki:** p. 126 (girl); **Shutterstock images**: p. 6 (top left: © Dmitry Meinikov), p. 7 (top left: © MANDY GODBEHEAR), p. 30, p. 48 (President Obama: Mistydawnphoto), p. 63 (top right: © Lightpoet), p. 71 (© Petrenko Andriy), p. 73 (photographer: © Radu Razvan, mobile phone: © vovan), p. 75 (top: © dusko, bottom: © Phase4Photography), p. 101 (© Eric Willmünder), p. 104 (left: © Elena Rostunova, right: © Piotr Marcinski), p. 106 (centre: © Lucian Coman), p. 114 (© Christofoto), p. 116 (centre: © Gary718), p. 117 (top: © Feng Yu), p. 118 (top: © John Schwegel), p. 121 (left: © Attila JÁNDI, right: © Rikko), p. 122 (© Iofoto), p. 123 (bottom right: © Kim Reinick), p. 125 (top left: © Kusma, top right: © Dimitriy Shironosov1, logs: © Jose AS Reyes, fish: © Evlakhov Valeriy, tiger: © neelsky), p. 126 (flag: © Dusan Po), p. 131 (top left: © Dave Massey, bottom left: © Eyes Talk, footprint: © kazberry, bottom right: Becky Stares), p. 132 (© AGphotographer), p. 134 (apple core: © Ivaschenko Roman), p. 139 (© Iakov Kalinin); **Sipa Press**, Paris: pp. 33-37 (© Olivier Jobard); **The Sun**, London: p. 66 (© 2008 The Sun / nisyndication.com); p. 82 (© 2007 The Sun / nisyndication.com); **WhatKidsCanDO / Santa Monica High School:** p. 112; **Wikimedia.org**: p. 21 (centre: http://commons.wikimedia.org/wiki/File:Campodetrabajo1.jpg)

Cover

Getty Images: © Christian Michaels